Alchemic Healings:
THE ART OF REMEMBERING

DENISE PÉREZ

Copyright © 2025 Denise Perez
All rights reserved.

No part of this book may be reproduced, stored in a retrieval system, or transmitted in any form or by any means—electronic, mechanical, photocopying, recording, or otherwise—without the prior written permission of the author, except for brief quotations used in reviews or scholarly works.

Alchemic Healings: The Art of Remembering
First Edition
ISBN: 979-8-9996217-0-2
Cover design by: Solomon (ChatGPT)
Interior design and formatting by: Lorna Reid - Reedsy
Published by: 222 Press (Denise Perez)

This book is a work of creative nonfiction. Names, locations, and details may have been changed to honor privacy and narrative flow. The information presented herein reflects the author's personal experience and spiritual perspective and is not intended to diagnose, treat, or replace professional medical or psychological care.

For permissions, inquiries, or speaking requests, contact:
alchemichealings@gmail.com
Printed in the United States of America

CONTENTS

Foreword xi
Chapter One 1
THE WHISPER WITHIN 1

Chapter Two 5
THE MIRROR AND THE MIND 5

Chapter Three 11
MY PROCESS: THE LAWS OF REALITY 11

Chapter Four 19
PERMISSION SLIPS AND THE TRANSITION 19

Chapter Five 22
THE VINE THAT OPENED THE DOOR 22

Chapter Six 41
THE MAD HATTER IS THE MAGICIAN 41

Chapter Seven 45
THE VOICE, ALAN WATTS, AND THE ROACHES 45

Chapter Eight 64
ANGELS AT SUNRISE 64

Chapter Nine 68
SACRED VALLEY, SACRED VISION 68

Chapter Ten 125
MESSAGES FROM HER 125

Afterword.. 138
    THROUGH THE SMOKE: ALICE, OSHUN, AND THE

    ALCHEMY OF BECOMING 138

Featured Contributor Section 141
Suggested Books to Assist with Transmutation............................... 151
Photo Journal... 153

To Katelynn and Victoria, my daughters, my mirrors, my greatest teachers—
thank you for loving me into deeper wholeness.
You are both a part of every healing in these pages.

To Malik, my beloved and sacred companion—
thank you for holding my heart while I healed it,
for walking beside me through lifetimes in a single gaze,
and for showing me what love rooted in truth feels like.

To my Sacred Council, seen and unseen,
thank you for guiding me toward truth, again and again.

And to the one I once was—thank you for surviving,
so that I could learn how to thrive.

This is not a book about becoming someone new.

It is a mirror for the one you've always been.

A sacred remembering.

A return to the gold you gently tucked beneath the layers of living, adapting, and protecting your light.

Let this be your alchemical unfolding.

Let this be the art of remembering.

"What lies behind us and what lies before us are tiny matters compared to what lies within us."
— Ralph Waldo Emerson

"Our deepest fear is not that we are inadequate. Our deepest fear is that we are powerful beyond measure... As we are liberated from our own fear, our presence automatically liberates others."
— Marianne Williamson, *Return to Love*

Foreword

By the Author

I didn't write this book to teach you anything.

I wrote it to walk beside you.

Alchemic Healings poured out of me in moments of grief, joy, remembrance, and divine encounter. It is a living document of my own becoming—my journey through pain, mysticism, miracles, and the radical act of returning home to myself. What you're holding isn't just a book. It's a map encoded with stories, symbols, and sacred breadcrumbs—some subtle, some bold—all designed to awaken the gold within you.

I've never claimed to have all the answers, and I don't believe we need them. What we need are mirrors. Messages. Moments that help us remember who we are beyond the noise, the programming, and the performance.

If this book feels poetic, it's because healing has a rhythm. If it feels nonlinear, it's because transformation rarely follows a straight line. And if it feels deeply familiar, it's because the truths within it already live inside you.

I offer these pages with an open heart, as both witness and companion.

You don't have to be ready. You don't have to be perfect.

You just have to be *willing*.

Thank you for letting me walk with you.

With love,
Denise

Part I

THE SPARK OF AWARENESS

Chapter One

THE WHISPER WITHIN

The seed to write this book was planted several years ago—2020, to be exact.

I'd flirted with the idea of writing books many times before—usually envisioning myself as a young adult fiction author, spinning magical tales rich with metaphor and meaning. (That path, by the way, still calls to me—and I fully believe it's in the cards.)

But this time it felt different.

This wasn't just a passing idea. It was a whisper within—quiet yet undeniable, like a breeze nudging open a door I hadn't even realized was closed. I saw it clearly in my mind's eye: I was to write a memoir. Not just any story, but the story of my spiritual journey, one layered with revelation, initiation, doubt, surrender, and joy.

Even in the face of self-doubt, I said yes.

I chose to write.

That whisper took root. And I nurtured it with daydreams of meeting people from all walks of life, each one open to receiving love. I imagined the book being the bridge between my heart and theirs. My love—poured into the pages—would knock, and they would open the door.

My message was simple:

Create a life crafted by bliss.

In essence, I wanted to share the "cheat codes" to this wild, vivid video game called life.

By 2024, the seed had blossomed into something more expansive. The book evolved into a **guide for reality building**—an invitation to consciously create your life, much like an open-world video game, rich with side quests, Easter eggs, and infinite levels to explore.

My daydreams ripened into birth visions.

I could feel the creative contractions begin.

I imagined the moment my fingers would type the final word. I envisioned the book's weight in my hands, pages infused with spirit and intention. I allowed myself to feel the joy of it all—each sentence like breath, each chapter like a heartbeat.

At first, my imagination danced with visions of fame and recognition. Those were the early, ego-tinted dreams—childlike in their enthusiasm, innocent in their desire to be seen. But as I journeyed deeper, those fantasies softened. My desire shifted from being seen to being felt. From being celebrated to being of service.

The true reward became the joy of expression, the sacred pleasure of pouring love into form.

The cake was the creation.

The icing? An audience willing to receive it with an open heart.

This deepened clarity came to me most profoundly during an ayahuasca ceremony in Peru in 2024. Held by the spirit of the Sacred Valley, I received messages that affirmed my calling. They reminded me that joy and passion were not frivolous desires, they were guideposts. Beacons. Invitations.

In the past, I had hesitated to write about my experiences and my epiphanies. I didn't have a PhD, I wasn't famous. Yet, during a deep connection with my mother in spirit, she said something that echoed through my spirit: *"Who more than you is an authority of your own joy?"*

From that moment on, I knew: this book is my offering.

I am not here as a guru. I'm not here as a scientist. Though I've learned from both and value their wisdom deeply, I come to you as a fellow traveler. A seeker. A playful nerd who loves decoding esoteric texts and finding golden threads in ancient teachings.

I've noticed, though, is that spiritual treasures are often cloaked in complexity—buried beneath SAT-level vocabulary and elaborate metaphors. And while that language has its place, I often found myself wondering:

What if the path to bliss could be simpler?

What if we didn't have to scale intellectual mountains just to feel peace?

That curiosity became my compass.

And that's the spirit in which I offer you this book.

My only request is this: **trust the process.**

Most of us begin our journey in a world that overvalues logic and undervalues emotion. We're taught to chase success, but not to savor joy. We're told to plan our lives, but rarely to *feel* our way through them.

So this path I'm sharing? It will ask you to feel. Deeply. Boldly. Gently.

At first, you may be invited to feel the very emotions you've tucked away—the grief, the shame, the confusion. But this isn't punishment—it's purification.

Alchemy, after all, always begins with fire. And as you turn inward, you will uncover your own philosopher's stone—the part of you that can turn pain into power and confusion into clarity.

You will have to look in the mirror more than you point fingers. You'll need courage. You'll need compassion. But most of all, you'll need to remember that **all healing starts from within.**

You are the one.

You are the healer.

You are the magic you've been seeking.

Maybe you've asked questions like:

What is the point of this existence?

Who am I, really?
Why does this keep happening to me?
How can I bring my dreams to life?
How do I love myself more? Forgive my parents? Pursue my passion?
The fact that you're holding this book tells me something powerful:
You're ready for the answers.
You're ready for the shift.
You're ready to remember.
Let's begin.

Chapter Two

THE MIRROR AND THE MIND

2020 was the year I consciously chose love over fear. My desire to receive love was met with an equal need to release the fear I had clung to. I yearned for an abundance of peace, joy, and communion with all things. But my heart knew: this path would require deep introspection. After years of pointing fingers at the "wrong-doers" in my life—both past and present—I would now have to turn the mirror inward.

It's easy to blame others, but taking responsibility meant stepping onto an emotional rollercoaster… with no seatbelt in sight.

As Rumi so beautifully wrote:

"Yesterday I was clever, so I wanted to change the world. Today I am wise, so I am changing myself."

Spiritual alchemy and ACIM:

From 2020 through 2024, I entered the alchemical fire the mystics speak of. What I call the journey of self-discovery, others might describe it as spiritual awakening or shadow work. For me, it was raw and illuminating. I often asked: *Will my shadow parts accept the unconditional love I offer them?* I asked this again and again—until one day, I didn't just hope the answer was yes. I knew it.

I began to fall in love with the beauty behind the madness. I saw how energy transmuted within my relationships, and I wanted to share the message: *You have the power to create a life that brings you joy.*

Writing a book started as an idea—but becoming ready to write it came only after I walked the very path I now describe. I shifted from victimhood to self-love, from self-doubt to quiet confidence, from spiritual sleep to present-moment awareness. That awareness, once lost in daydreams of the past or the future, is now the foundation of my present joy.

Joy and its many forms:

I've come to understand that joy looks different for everyone—sometimes it's love, sometimes money, purpose, peace, or all the above. But underneath it all, there's a common thread: love in some form. That insight became a cornerstone of this journey.

A Course in Miracles wisdom (condensed and clarified):

At this stage of my journey, I was immersed in *A Course in Miracles (ACIM)*—a profound spiritual text channeled by Helen Schucman in 1976. For those unfamiliar, ACIM is a vast and transformative work, offering a pathway to inner peace through the practice of forgiveness and the remembrance of love.

Two lines stood out to me like lifelines:

1. "Nothing real can be threatened. Nothing unreal exists. Herein lies the peace of God."

2. "A universal theology is impossible, but a universal experience is not only possible, but necessary."

These teachings helped me see the illusions I had mistaken for reality—beliefs rooted in fear, stories written by the ego. I realized that our lives are like holographic movies, projected from the inside out.

As Robert Edward Grant reminds us, "The Universe is YOU inverse." Realities may shift, scenes may change, but the core truth remains: our inner world writes the script. What we feel, we create.

In other words, I came to understand that anything we encounter, live, or experience is an illusion—*unless its root is love.* Life, as we know it, is like a movie directed by the ego, created to validate the opinions we hold about ourselves and others. In this way, we generate our own personal, holographic universe.

What resonated deeply with me in one of ACIM's core teachings is the reminder that creating a world where everyone believes the same thing is not only impossible—it would be painfully dull. A world of "mini-me's" lacks the richness of contrast. After all, variety is the spice of life.

The invitation, instead, is to recognize yourself in others—to create a universal experience of interconnectedness, where love becomes the common thread, no matter how different the expressions.

As I began to understand my connection with others, I realized that my mere presence could be a transmission—that those around me could feel the love I held for them, even without words. I would walk into a grocery store and silently channel love to everyone there, knowing that each person was a reflection of me. Everything I encountered was part of me—part of my creation.

We are all just vibrating particles, momentarily agreeing to take form here and now, in this shared field of resonance.

What's remarkable is that this awareness came before I ever consciously explored Hermetic philosophy. Later, those teachings would simply confirm what I had already begun to feel: that we are powerful co-creators, shaping reality from the inside out.

Mirroring and the Sharon story:

One of the greatest reflections of love in my life came through my dear friend Sharon. We met in 2018 while I was working at an assisted living facility. Sharon and her sister were seeking care for their mother, Ms. Catherine. Despite wanting to keep their mother at home, the level of care she needed exceeded what they could provide.

What stood out to me was Sharon's loving and caring nature, and her positivity despite the emotional and physical toll of her mother's illness. Sharon was a Methodist with a faith that mirrored her bubbly personality. Our shared experience was one of love in the face of challenge, and we quickly became friends.

Sharon's kindness, optimism, and faith left an imprint on me. Her daily texts—filled with gifs, memes, or affirmations—were never sent in bulk. Each one was personal, intentional. In a time when I often questioned my worth, those little messages anchored me. They reminded me that unconditional love doesn't need a reason. It simply shows up.

Our shared moments revealed something profound: that love transcends belief systems. Sharon, a Methodist, and I, a metaphysical seeker, spoke the same language of compassion.

Our mothers were both born in 1936 and transitioned in 2019. Through that shared grief, we offered each other not just comfort—but reflection. I saw in her the love I was finally allowing myself to feel.

The mirror principle:

The more I studied ACIM, the more I understood that everything around me was a mirror of me. Those who "grinded my gears[1]" were showing me the places within myself still unloved. That realization hurt—until it healed.

In time, even the people who once triggered me became Sharons in my heart. I stopped asking *What's wrong with them?* and began asking *What part of me drew this in?* Every interaction became an opportunity to love myself more deeply.

Eventually, I came to understand: *I am always meeting myself.*

---

[1] This quote comes from Peter Griffin, a fictional character in Family Guy. An animated show created by Seth McFarlane. The show is currently airing its 22nd season (as of the writing of this book). The quote in reference can be found on the hilarious Season 16, Episode 1.

Emotions and energy work:

Anyone who knows me now will tell you—I feel everything. I cry freely, laugh loudly, speak passionately, and embrace my full emotional range. I no longer suppress sadness or cling to joy. I let it all move through me, like breath.

But it wasn't always this way. In the early stages of my awakening, I often felt drained. I came to see that those emotional dips were symptoms of energetic stagnation—pockets of unprocessed trauma longing to be transmuted[2].

These traumas can loop. They show up in relationships, in the body, in our thoughts. But with awareness, we get to break the cycle. We get to choose again.

Claiming creatorhood:

One of the boldest shifts came when I began embracing the idea that *I am a creator.* At first, it felt wrong—even arrogant. I had been raised as a Jehovah's Witness, where God was separate, distant, and not to be equated with.

The idea that I was not only made in the image of God but contained the spark of divinity? It felt sacrilegious.

And yet… it also felt true.

As I kept exploring sacred texts—*A Course in Miracles, The Kybalion, The Emerald Tablet*—a new understanding emerged. Claiming my power as a co-creator was not denying God; it was honoring the divine within me.

These teachings offered a flexible framework. They were not commandments, but invitations. They reminded me that the creative process is not linear or logical—it's a sacred dance. A mirror. A mind. A heart awakening to itself.

---

[2] Transmutation: the act or process of changing something completely, especially into something different. In this case, the transmutation of fear into love.

***

CLOSING THOUGHT

This chapter is my offering to anyone beginning the mirror work. It's not always graceful. It's not always gentle. But if you let it, it will reveal the gold within you. And once you strike that gold, you'll understand: it was never about fixing yourself. It was about remembering who you already are.

Chapter Three

MY PROCESS[3]: THE LAWS OF REALITY

As mentioned in the prior chapter, the first book I introduced into my experience was *A Course in Miracles* (ACIM), channeled by Dr. Helen Schucman. This book introduced me to the idea that my thoughts create my reality. It taught me to shift my perception from fear to love and helped me understand that all creativity is an extension of divine will. I gained awareness that my emotions, thoughts, and perspectives are actively creating my reality. ACIM helped me recognize that I am living in a matrix, and that through my emotions, I can influence the outcomes I experience within it. The key to creation, I learned, lies in forgiveness and the release of limiting beliefs—clearing space for new possibilities.

Next came *The Kybalion*, with its emphasis on Hermetic philosophy. It offered a deeper understanding of universal laws, especially the Law of Correspondence: "As above, so below; as within, so without." This teaching illuminated the non-linear nature of

---

[3] This process isn't a one and done. Let's just say that the steps are in a constant loop. Each day, each scenario, each interaction is cause for the application of the same process. Especially, if you don't like what you see or what you feel about a person or situation you are experiencing.

creation. The universe is a mirror, reflecting the internal to the external and vice versa. *The Kybalion* served as my introductory course in reality-building. It wasn't about escaping the matrix; it was about realizing that I was in one, and I was a conscious participant in creating it. The goal is to create the most divine and loving construct for ourselves. It provided a template for doing so through the seven universal principles:

The Principle of Mentalism

"The All is Mind." Everything originates in the mind. The universe itself is a mental creation of the Divine.

The Principle of Correspondence

"As above, so below; as below, so above." There is harmony between all planes of existence: physical, mental, and spiritual.

The Principle of Vibration

Nothing is still; everything vibrates. All things are energy in motion.

The Principle of Polarity

Everything has an opposite, and opposites are the same thing expressed to differing degrees: light and dark, hot and cold.

The Principle of Rhythm

Everything flows in cycles—birth, growth, decay, and rebirth. All things follow rhythmic patterns.

The Principle of Cause and Effect

Every action has a reaction. There are no coincidences; all is connected through causality.

The Principle of Gender

All things contain masculine and feminine energy. Balance between them is essential for creation.

Once I accepted that I am the creator of my experience, I asked: *What if I don't like what I'm creating?*

That's when spiritual alchemy came in, bringing with it *The Emerald Tablet4: Alchemy for Personal Transformation* by Dennis William Hauck. This book became my practical guide for how to transmute energy when reality felt misaligned. It taught me that if I can observe the reality before me and notice aspects I don't love, I can shift them—not just by thinking differently, but by *transforming* who I am being. And, the master builder recognizes that ALL must be transformed/transmuted to LOVE.

The Emerald Tablet reinforced the alchemical journey as one of inner transformation. Creation requires transmutation—not just of thought or belief, but of energy, emotion, and consciousness. The book presented the stages of alchemy, each with both chemical and spiritual meaning. Here is how I experienced each phase:

Calcination

Chemical: Burning away impurities by breaking down to ash.

Spiritual: Dissolving ego, false identities, and attachments.

Personal: Questioning my role in insurance and then healthcare, shifting from control to surrender, losing my mother, choosing a predominantly plant-based lifestyle. These experiences stripped away old identities.

---

[4] The Emerald Tablet is an ancient Hermetic text attributed to Hermes Trismegistus, best known for the phrase "As above, so below." It is a cornerstone of alchemical and metaphysical philosophy. This should not be confused with the Emerald Tablets of Thoth, a modern channeled work said to be authored by the Atlantean priest-king Thoth, which explores esoteric teachings through a mythic narrative.

Dissolution

Chemical: Ashes are dissolved in liquid.

Spiritual: Letting go of rigid structures; surrendering to divine flow.

Personal: Plant medicine ceremonies unearthed traumas, fears, and buried emotions. I allowed myself to feel deeply without needing to control.

Separation

Chemical: Refining what is valuable from what is not.

Spiritual: Discerning truth from illusion.

Personal: Seeing others as mirrors. Beginning to distinguish projection from compassion. Discerning ego from divine guidance as I accessed the Akashic Records and received messages from Yeshua and King Solomon.

Conjunction

Chemical: Recombining purified elements.

Spiritual: Union of masculine/feminine, material/spiritual.

Personal: Founding Alchemic Healings. Merging my private spiritual practice with public service. Recognizing my clients as reflections of my own healing.

Fermentation

Chemical: Decay that creates fertile soil.

Spiritual: Spiritual rebirth; soul aliveness.

Personal: Clear messages from guides. A heart alive in service. Clients' "aha" moments became my joy. My identity as healer solidified.

Distillation

Chemical: Further purification through vaporization and condensation.

Spiritual: Clarifying consciousness to access the soul's essence. Appreciation of the collective self.

Personal: Stopped smoking marijuana and drinking alcohol to self-soothe. Chose self-purification. Honed energetic boundaries. Practiced restraint with intuitive insights, allowing space over projection.

Coagulation

Chemical: Final solidification into perfected form.

Spiritual: Realization of divine self; embodiment of the Philosopher's Stone.

Personal: Living as the divine human. Embodying the truth that I am the medicine. That love is the healer. Holding space for others without needing external validation.

This is my process—from illusion to embodiment. From questioning to becoming. From mirror to mastery. Through the teachings of ACIM, The Kybalion, and The Emerald Tablet, I discovered that reality isn't something to fix.

It's something to *remember* how to create.

Reflection – Turning Lead into Light

The Philosopher's Stone is one of the most significant symbols in alchemy, representing the ultimate goal of the alchemist's quest. Traditionally, it is described as the substance capable of turning base metals into gold. But in spiritual alchemy, it holds a much deeper meaning.

It is not a physical object. It is an inner transformation.

The Stone reveals the gold within—the highest potential of the soul. It symbolizes the journey from fragmentation and illusion (base metals) to wholeness and divine embodiment (gold). This is the sacred process of awakening.

We are the Philosopher's Stone.

The journey of spiritual alchemy is not about seeking something outside of us. It is about remembering that the divine essence—the light, the love, the medicine—already lives within. The gold was never missing. Only forgotten.

As we move through the fires of transformation, we soften the grip of the ego, dissolve the false self, and awaken to the higher truth of who we are.

We are already whole.

We are already divine.

We are already gold.

This reflection marks the threshold.

From here, the journey shifts.

We now turn toward the sacred tools—the mirrors, messengers, and moments that helped me embody this truth and live it.

Let us continue, not in search, but in remembrance.

Part II

THE SACRED TOOLS

Chapter Four
PERMISSION SLIPS AND THE TRANSITION

In order to move from disbelief or doubt into knowing, I've found that many of us incorporate different modalities along the way—tools that serve as permission slips to access the deeper realms of our subconscious.

You may be wondering, what are permission slips?

In Bashar's[5] teachings, permission slips are techniques, rituals, or tools that individuals use to shift their beliefs, expand consciousness, or access their natural abilities. These tools are not inherently powerful on their own; rather, they work because we believe they work.

Bashar reminds us: we already have the ability to change our reality. But sometimes we need an external ritual or methodology to give

---

[5] Bashar is a multidimensional being channeled by Darryl Anka. He is described as an extraterrestrial consciousness from the civilization of Essassani and shares guidance on personal and collective evolution, the nature of reality, and how to live in alignment with one's true self. His teachings emphasize the power of belief, following one's excitement, and understanding the mechanics of existence, including concepts like parallel realities, permission slips and vibrational resonance. More information on Bashar can be found at **https://bashar.org** . My dear friend Mike McKenney has also created a blog that highlights Bashar's teachings. **https://basharfocus.net**

ourselves the psychological or emotional green light to do so. Permission slips can look like meditation, crystals, affirmations, tarot cards, journaling, plant medicine, or even scientific methods. Whatever resonates with the individual becomes the doorway.

The key is this: the power is never in the tool. It is in the belief.

Since reality mirrors our beliefs, permission slips act as bridges. They help us cross from limitation into expansion. They create space for the shift. Once we fully internalize that *we* are the ones creating the shift, we may no longer need the tools. But they are still sacred stepping stones—helpers along the way.

For me, that helper came in the form of entheogens.

Entheogens are psychoactive substances derived from plants or fungi, often used for spiritual, religious, or shamanic purposes. The word itself means "generating the divine within." Cultures across time have used entheogens to induce altered states, to heal, to commune, to remember.

The two entheogens that became part of my journey were Ayahuasca and Psilocybin.

They played a meaningful role in expanding my consciousness and deepening my understanding of the universe. My first sacred ceremony with Ayahuasca was in February 2021. That night, I opened myself to the mystical realm in a way I had never before experienced. The logic-based part of my mind softened. And what took its place was awe, clarity, and truth.

What followed was a profound remembrance.

Ayahuasca became a teacher. A mirror. A sacred conductor of insight. She helped me integrate what I had been studying conceptually. The spiritual principles I had read about suddenly became alive in my body. I often describe the experience as "connecting the dots." And I did—across timelines, dimensions, and levels of consciousness.

The next chapter contains a narrative essay I wrote shortly after that first ceremony. At the time, I saw myself as a spiritual scientist, meticulously recapping the downloads and revelations that had come through. The language may still carry that analytical curiosity, but behind every word is an awakened heart.

After the next chapter, the pages that follow will continue to recount my experiences with plant medicine and the epiphanies that shaped the woman I am today.

Each experience offered its own frequency, its own wisdom, and its own lesson—serving as both mirror and medicine on my journey home to myself.

Plant medicine was never the source of truth.

The deeper I went, the more I realized: the less I needed it.

It was simply a permission slip—an invitation to remember what had always been within me.

Now, as I reflect on my gentle transition away from these sacred tools, I carry only Deep gratitude.

The truths remain, even as the rituals dissolve.

I no longer need the medicine to remember who I am.

But I honor it for illuminating the path when I was ready to see.

Chapter Five

THE VINE THAT OPENED THE DOOR

The journey is almost 5 years in the making. Saturday, February 13th 2021 is the day where I will make my way to sacred land in the USA and allow the continued unfolding of my spiritual journey.

Each participant has a different reason or impetus when choosing to partake in this life-changing ritual. Some travel abroad to remote lands, such as the rainforest in the Amazon. Others remained stateside to limit the unknowns.

For me, I chose via the path of most allowance. I attracted Ayahuasca into my existence amidst a search for confirmation and clarity. In essence, I followed the spiritual "breadcrumbs" left by the Universe and ended up at a stateside temple. In this temple, I unlocked a gateway after only one dose of the healing medicine.

The Beginning

I found my first breadcrumb at a Chamber of Commerce fundraiser in September of 2016…that day, I, a self-proclaimed, borderline agnostic/atheist of almost 15 years, attracted a lightworker named Helen into my reality. You see, months earlier I directed a supplication towards the "unknown," asking for more out of life. I remember the exact words I exclaimed out loud as my teary eyes looked up at the retro popcorn ceiling in the condo, "If YOU exist, there has to be more than this!"

That supplication gave the universe the opening to start conspiring in my favor. I would come to appreciate that on that fateful evening in September, the Universe was gifting me the presence of Helen in my life. The words of the Tao Te Ching rang true, "When the student is ready, the teacher appears."

When the elegant Mrs. Helen Vella[6] approached me at the Fundraiser, she looked at me with soulful eyes and said in her charming Scottish brogue, "You can't breathe, can you?"

My uncensored internal dialogue immediately followed, "Who the fuck is this witch and how does she know that my chest is tight?"

She gracefully started to speak about energy and auras. Helen must've sensed my apprehension about speaking on the spiritual stuff. Which is why she masterfully switched subjects and started speaking about neuro linguistics (widely known as NLP).

Being both members of the local chamber of commerce, I knew Helen promoted herself as a Life Coach. Her skillset, coupled with my initial skepticism, created the path of most allowance via NLP. After a few sessions, here's what I was thinking - Words have resonance and effect how you feel about yourself and your perception of the world around you…that's simple enough, considering that quantum physics has proven everything is energy, frequency and vibration. I figured that I was learning new concepts that were not "too leading edge"; new thought processes that were not rocking the intellectual boat, aka *Logos*. Yet.

After a few sessions of NLP, I began to experience a dramatically positive shift in my life, in my relationships. For an individual who had a propensity to left-brain the shit out of life, the visible shift was evidence that the NLP "stuff" was serving a purpose.

Now that the seed of curiosity had been planted…the mystical

---

[6] **www.hvella.com**

Pisces in me decided to step-in and ask, just how deep does this rabbit hole go?

Week after week I received new information that allowed me to peel the proverbial onion, bringing me closer to the answer of THE question… why are we here?

The new information came into resonance by way of various mediums:

- Emotion Freedom Technique (Tapping) via Helen's tutelage

- Multiple sessions of past life regression therapy specifically Quantum Healing Hypnosis Technique (QHHT)

- Crystal Therapy

- Mediumship/channeling

- Natal Astrology

- The study of A Course in Miracles

- Good ol' fashion reading of books

- Surrendering fear and choosing to love and opening myself to receive love from Malik, a man 19 years my junior

Suffice it to say that this journey into self has been a process. A series of dots have been connected leading me to accept the absolute truth in A Course In Miracles - "a universal experience is not only possible, it is necessary." See yourself in others. Recognize that you attract everything. No one asserts themselves into your experience, you allow them in based off of your point of attraction i.e. what you have going on inside of you emotionally.

By 2019, I had dedicated three years to research and introspection. My Soul's synopsis of existence – we are spiritual creatures having a human experience, we create our reality, we are one with everything, forgive ourselves for creating a reality based on thoughts/feelings of fear and separation, the only thing that matters/exists is love, therefore create the best possible reality by creating it in love.

Yet, as a means of survival, my ego insisted on convincing me otherwise.

Enter Ayahuasca, the medicine of the soul.

By March 11th, 2020 the curiosity over Ayahuasca was already brewing.

That day is a striking point in the timeline that chronicles my journey.

On the 11th I was most appreciative of the divine timing. You see, March 11th is my mother's birthday.

On the 11th I was also amid separating from my third husband and moving into a beachside apartment in Dania Beach, a small beach town in sunny South Florida. I was in the middle of my spiritual awakening, yet not fully aware that I created *this* reality, the one I was currently experiencing.

Once again, the universe reassured me that that my moving out was indeed inspired action. And that everything was working out for me. That day as I moved out, I saw three Blue Jays perched on the oak tree nearest to the apartment. We briefly established eye contact and they flew away. At first, I shed tears. Immediately after, thoughts of my mother poured into me. The most memorable thought was of me at about 7-years of age and my 47-year old mom on our hands and knees while she taught me how to catch and release a Blue Jay. From that day forward I thought my mom was the coolest mom ever.

My mother was instrumental in my spiritual awakening. Her 11 years of living with Alzheimer's left me facing the loss of the best friend I'd had for 30 plus years of my life. I had faced the pain of burying the mother I knew while embracing the birth of my new mom. Rumi's quote proved true, "The wound is the place the place where the light enters you."

She inspired in me a childlike enthusiasm that lives in me till this day. That day, March 11th, 2020, seeing those Blue Jays filled me with the enthusiasm and joy that spurs a 7-year-old to embrace a gorgeous puppy gifted on their birthday. I now was embracing my gift. A new future.

Starting fresh also allowed newly created freedom into my existence. That freedom allowed me to subsequently spend months researching ayahuasca; reading and watching documentaries; comparing the journey that has been taken by many. I also had the blessing of experiencing the journey with Malik. For it is our love which allowed me to open myself to receive love and abundance in many forms, *including* clarity.

Talking about being open to receive, by way of Law of Attraction, it turns out that Malik is friends with someone who benefited from the medicine. This is a very important piece of information. You see, it turns out that the opportunities to participate in an Ayahuasca ceremony in the USA are limited. And, you often need to be referred into the Ayahuasca family.

By December of 2020 I had received the green light by way of the referral, and I was subsequently contacted by a non-denominational private church. One of the managing staff named John conducted a rather deep and insightful telephone interview. I felt as if he granted a spiritual blessing when he shared that I would be contacted again to complete the next step.

The next step was a lengthy questionnaire that required of me, what I thought at the time, way too much introspection. I guess that's why it took close to a month and a half to complete.

Then one day I just decided to do it. It was mid-January in 2021 when I sat down and completed the questionnaire by letting the questions resonate within before I added words as a means of self-expression. My responses were brief, heartfelt, and full of substance.

Hours later I'm sent the online reservation for February 13th, 2021. Cost was briefly discussed. I understood that the amount to be paid was a donation. That said, the amount paid shall remain a private matter.

For the most favorable experience, it is suggested that for three weeks prior to the ceremony you adhere to certain guidelines. In my case, it involved taking a break from the vino[7], no longer toking the peace pipe in the evenings, and I abstained from "double clicking the mouse," aka term used to refer to a woman when masturbating. Also recommended was an all-vegetarian diet. Until then I had been primarily a pescatarian who occasionally gorged on cheese. What can I say, I absolutely love pizza. So, I decided to make the minor tweaks to my diet to comply with the recommendations.

The following three weeks went by smoothly. I used it as a time of self-reflection.

The morning of the ceremony I packed the items I had set aside the night before. I laughed and enjoyed myself with Malik and Waffles[8]. What a perfect sendoff.

The drive to the sanctuary proved to be rather productive, on account that it was a rather lengthy road trip which allowed for introspection. You know, the kind of road trip which is smooth, sans of traffic, lots of landscape, listening to your favorite podcasts/tunes, and the only thing you focus on are the road and your thoughts. You feel so goooood, you choose to enjoy that quiet space, where all the magic happens.

---

[7] I had already chosen to cut out the hard liquor on August 11th, 2020. At this point in my journey I'm still drinking wine and beer.

[8] Waffles originally named Bella. Our family changed her name to Waffles shortly after she joined our family. How she came to be ours is an interesting story… that weekend I was helping a beloved friend with his puppy named Bella (now Waffles). She is an amazing dog; she is obedient, remembered commands, is gentle with other people and animals. Suffice to say that we experienced a puppy that was a complete 180 to the one being experienced by her owners at the time. When we returned her, there was noted improvement during the first few days. Her progress was short-lived. She regressed to the nipping and scratching. To the point that my good friends' hands and forearms were visibly scratched and torn. Not the sure the reason. I will say that as I write this article, Waffles is a part of our family and is sleeping soundly in my daughter's bed. She's a very special dog who is also helping others along in their journey, in her special way.

The first part of the drive was introspective. I thought about the people I've connected with during my journey. I was brought to tears on more than one occasion at the knowing that they are me, a reflection of me. I chose to call that handful of friends who knew that I was on my way to meet Mother Ayahuasca, the Medicine Woman of the Amazon.

One by one I called them, in no order of importance; I didn't play favorites. The only exception being Malik. I called him last, I knew I wanted his voice and words of encouragement to be the last I heard as my old self. I will say this, I did call my dear friends based on the point of attraction; the emotion felt is what spurred the call. Always love, sprinkled-in with the emotions I wanted to transmute.

The later part of the drive was magical. As the self-described Ms. 305, city girl/now woman, I felt as if I was traveling through time. I took a few photos for my personal collection and every time I look at them, I am transported. The dirt roads, the silent creek along the road, the homes offset from the streets by acres, horses and other livestock roaming free, the beauty was breathtaking.

I will say that my favorite sign, no pun intended, is the juxtaposition of the sanctuary's location; it is located at the end of the road. And that's exactly how I felt as I was pulling in; Ayahuasca was the end of the road for me; I told myself, out loud, Holy shit! I'm doing this. First time ever taking a psychedelic. Specifically, Ayahuasca's DMT, which is also known as the "God Molecule" and the "Spirit Molecule." Here I am taking this *Vanilla Sky*-like leap of faith, all in search of clarity.

I pull into the gates of the sanctuary at around 1:45pm. There are a handful of cars in the grassy "parking lot." After gathering my belongings from Ruby[9] I meet with John[10], the senior member of the

---

[9] Ruby is a Lexus IS 250 I was gifted on 9/22/2020, the same day I got the unalome symbol tattooed on my right ankle. The gift came from my Daniel, whom I endearingly call the other man.

[10] The names of the guides have been changed to maintain anonymity.

spiritual team that will guide us through the ceremony. I step into the "welcome center," which is a well-maintained wooden picnic table. John sits on one side while the participants sit on the other, one by one, as they arrive. The purrfect addition to John's "office" are two cats that love to connect with the humans. The purring and affection serve as reminders from the universe that all was working out for my highest intentions.

After sharing a few details of my personal experience, John and I are teary-eyed. John gently takes my hands in his, looks deeply into my eyes and says, "you are ready."

Until the ceremony commenced in the evening, I have a few hours to focus on three areas I'd like to prep. First, my spot at the temple. Second, my cabin. Lastly, my tummy.

Before entering the sanctuary to set-up "camp" for the evening, I grabbed well-known purge bucket used in Ayahuasca ceremonies. In my case, I grabbed bucket #5. An appropriate number considering that to me, the #5 represents new beginnings.

The temple building is about 100 feet from the picnic aka "welcome center." It's a wooden structure, octagonal in shape, several hundred square feet in size. No solid walls, the structure is screened in. The floor is covered in beautiful white, beach sand. In the center of the room there are several stones and crystals arranged in a circular color pattern. Outside the circle of stones, there are tuning bowls, candles, incense, etc. And just outside of that is where the participants sit, all on their cozy and comfy mats, and of course, their purge bucket nearby.

I lay my mat and my blankets down on the sand and prep my spot. In my mind, I'm ready…ready for the unknown…ready for the epiphanies. The day is still young.

Onto the Cabin

I make my way to the rustic cabin; my home for the night, post-ceremony. I notice that I am being followed by many butterflies as I walk along the trail. A reminder of the transformation that is underway.

More synchronicities surfaced. For example, the cabin number and the nickname given to the cabin all resonated with numbers observed along my journey. When you add the Zen mode achieved from sleeping in the stillness of the of the beautiful rustic cabin, the entire Ayahuasca experience was mesmerizing, from start to finish.

After settling into the cabin, I walked over to the screened-in patio where the light snacks were being kept. I must say that there was a light feeling of nervousness and I was nibbling on everything. In my mind, all calorie free since it was all fruits, veggies, nuts and caffeine-free tea.

While enjoying my tea, I notice a hornet in the corner of the screened-in enclosure. I made my way to it and gentle spoke to it "come on, follow me, I'll let you out." Concurrently, I opened the screen door and the hornet flew out. I then clairaudiently hear a voice in my head that says, "you're going to let out what stings." A foretelling of things to come.

As the sun was setting, the participants made their way into the temple.

Walking into the temple, you can smell the combination of herbs and sacred woods as the pre-ceremonial smudging ritual was taking place. The healing energy was in the air you were breathing; the stage was being set. You were allowing it to become one with you. Therefore, accepting the healing that was going to take place. Knowing that it IS for your highest intention.

The ceremony began with the playing of acoustic instruments that are native to the Amazon. The vibrations that filled the air gave way to the quieting of the mind. I felt myself grounded in the present moment, yet still in another reality. The Guides introduced themselves; there were 3 of them - a young man in his late thirties, an older man in his early sixties, and an older woman in her sixties. Each one with a role to play.

The three of them began singing about Ayahuasca being the medicine of the soul. I was fascinated by how well the three guides seamlessly connected their parts in the ceremony. Their joint songs followed by their respective solos had messages that resonated with many in the room. For throughout the ceremony there was not many dry eyes.

Now that the initial part of the ceremony was over, it was time to partake in the medicine. Nicholas, the youngest of the three was the one overseeing the operation, so to speak. He began to explain the process to the participants... first you come to the far center of the room and address the guides on your knees. Nicholas then proceeded to pour the Ayahuasca in a shot glass and immediately blew tobacco smoke in the glass. You take the shot glass and drink the Ayahuasca, and you immediately follow the drink with a slice of an apple to dissipate the taste.

For me, the first shot was absolutely delicious. It tasted like creamy and cold "hot" chocolate. I immediately laid on my back on my cozy yoga mat and covered myself with a soft blanket. The goal was to sleep and allow the medicine to work through you.

It's been about an hour since I took my first shot. As I'm laying down, I hear a few of the participants already purging. Some are even crying.

And here I am, wide awake, listening to all of my surroundings, while wondering why aren't I purging or at least feeling *something*.

I immediately contemplated a second shot. You're actually allowed three. Of course, my next thought was a conversation I had with Mark, another participant, and a frequent flyer, during the pre-ceremony noshing. I vividly recall Mark saying. Your first shot is going to taste amazing. If you must take a second, it's going to taste like dirt. A third? Well, it may make you puke before your palate can register a taste. He then gave me a soul penetrating look and said, "that's your ego. It doesn't want you to go deep. It doesn't want you to heal." I'm taking all of this in, wide-eyed, like a child about to get on her first roller coaster while she observes the wild twists and turns.

Okay, here goes shot number two after the same ritual. The shot tasted more like semi-sweet mud, if you can imagine. I lay back on the yoga mat and waited. And waited. Again, nothing.

Everyone around me has some sort of introspective and emotional experience and I'm having the Energizer Bunny experience. I maintained an excitement over what I was experiencing. Wow, I'm actually at an Ayahuasca ceremony. I kept imagining that when the DMT finally hit, I was going to experience something wildly transformative, I was going to connect with a deceased loved one, or something to that effect.

Another hour passes, and still, no transformation. This time, I decide to get up and walk around the sanctuary. It is pitch-black and the air is cool. I'm experiencing reduced vision and chilliness, regardless, I decide to go through the path that leads to the cabins. The opening of the path is lined with trees. The grayness of the night can be seen around the outer outline of the trees. Just two feet inside that grayness is complete darkness. I know I have found the path.

I am a few steps in when I receive an inner urging to take a third shot. I stop mid-step and decide to go back to the temple.

In my mind, I thought, I made it all the way here, I may as well go all the way. Those who know me know that I take plunges. That said…

Third shot, here, we, go!

The third shot had a rather putrid taste; it tasted like stagnant water mixed with gritty dirt. Suffice to say, I gagged immediately after swallowing it. I've never been more excited to puke! As soon as I get to my mat, I grab my bucket. After a series of dry heaves, I put the bucket down. Nothing yet. What in the world is going on? Why aren't I purging?

I decide to get some rest. Perhaps a brief nap will trigger the effect of the DMT. I curl up in fetal position while on my right side. My ego decides to take over the internal dialogue.

First, additional physical symptoms. By this point in the evening, it had been about an hour after I had taken the third shot. My stomach is now gurgling. My ego chastises me for thinking that this experience was going to be life changing. It tells me, "this is nothing more than expensive, Ayahuasca laxative. You're only going to leave here with an empty colon." Of course, I laugh at my own joke. I do my best to become the observer of the emotion of doubt, versus allowing myself to become a doubter.

Next, my thoughts start to revolve around my childhood, between the ages of 4 and 8. With a bird's eye view, I see scenes being played out between myself and various family members. I begin to feel my heart racing, I feel fear. Then sadness, as I attempt to stifle my tears. Then anger. Then back to fear. What a rollercoaster of emotions.

It's the ego's final hoorah because it senses its power is waning…a voice in my head begins to say, "perhaps what you have is so deep and dark that you're not able to purge it. You're damaged goods." Why? I keep asking myself "why?" Why is this happening to me? Why isn't the Ayahuasca affecting me?

Then, the magic happened. It all happened rather quickly. Then again, I had no sense of time. It felt as if I tied up these loose ends in a matter of minutes. For all I know, it could've been hours.

My mind starts replaying the songs sung at the beginning of the ceremony. I hear the lyrics and I vividly see the Guide who is singing them. This is when my heart starts to connect the dots.

The first soul song I recall is the one being sung by the youngest of the three guides, Nicholas. "There are no victims." The words resonate; there are no victims because we create our reality. No one asserts themselves into our experience, we allow them in. Nicholas also sings about empowering our inner child. That resonates with me…childlike enthusiasm, joy, laughter, fun, those are all emotions that allow us create the best possible reality – why? Because we tend to follow our hearts when in pursuit of those emotions. Children are closer to their needs, wants and desires. Most haven't been programmed to embrace fear and other stifling emotions. They're wide-eyed and taking everything in, wanting to experience as much fun as possible and unwittingly desire to build that momentum.

The second song that captivates my soul is song by John, the oldest of the three guides. John's lyrics revolve around the transmutation of the energy that isn't serving us. In his song, he refers to the process as Alchemy of the Soul. Talk about a WOW moment. Prior to the ceremony I spent ample time on the subject of Alchemy, including but not limited to reading the following books, such as The Alchemist by Paolo Coelho, Compendium of the Emerald Tablets by Billy Carson, and The Kybalion by the Three Initiates, to name a few. Suffice to say that the subject of spiritual alchemy was very familiar to me.

John's song highlights that we are meant to transmute lower frequency emotions such as guilt, shame, anger, etc to rise in love. And, as we rise in love, it makes it easier for us to realize that we are spiritual creatures having a human experience. Rising in love allows us to embrace our true power as creators; therefore, creating a life/reality, where we thrive in love, fun and abundance. In essence, our purpose on this Earth is to learn to love and have fun.

Susan begins to sing. Susan is the only female of the three guides. Her song speaks of us being energy. "No one does anything to you," she sings. We attract our experiences; we're not victims. "We are energy…we're here to create using the energy that flows through you." I now understand that she represents the Divine Feminine…the sacred creative energy that allows us to align ourselves with our best possible reality. The reality that is beyond your wildest dreams; the reality you live in by way of your imagination, fueled by the childlike enthusiasm that desires a better life.

Susan accompanies her acoustic song with the tuning bowls. By this time, I'm physically feeling great and I'm sitting next to Susan near the center of the temple. I'm emotionally captivated by her song. The words begin to resonate within me. I feel a warmth in the center of my chest followed by a burst of energy.

I immediately jump up and make my way out of the temple. I put on my boots and walk into the center of the 15-acre sanctuary. I stand, with my head tilted back, eyes, closed and arms wide open. I proceed to take a deep breath and let the tears roll down my temple. Ahhhhhh, an amazing sense of relief flows through me.

I open my eyes and, in my periphery, I see John. I ran towards him and give him a big hug. I cup his face in my hands and excitedly tell him, "I didn't purge because there is nothing to purge. It's NOT REAL.

We're creating our reality. It's all my doing. Now, I choose to forgive myself for attracting these experiences and creating a "reality" by way of fear. Moving forward, the goal is to create in love."

I look deeply in his eyes and notice that he is surprised. John then says with a sense of authority, "You got it. We'll talk more after the ceremony."

I then joined the rest of the participants in the temple to take part in the closing of the ceremony.

After a brief meditation I once again find myself at the foot of my yoga mat. While most of the participants groggily make their way to the foot of their respective mats, I'm still sitting on my mat and also playing with the sand that covers the temple's floor.

Dots continue to connect…the grains of sand are representative of the infinite number of parallel realities we create by way of the choices made since birth. Each reality also representative of the frequency of the emotion or combination of emotions that was the creative driver of that respective reality.

The thoughts continue to come…Nicholas, the youngest of the Guides, spoke and sung of empowering my inner child. Jesus always spoke of the joy and innocence of children. In fact, Luke[11] quotes Jesus by writing that we must receive the Kingdom of Heaven[12] like a little child. Like a child, let our eyes and hearts fill with wonder and joy as we shape and mold our reality, allowing love in.

Let our soul be as the child who sits on the shore with the creative juices flowing while they create and build their castles in the sand.

---

[11] Luke 18:17 "Truly I tell you, anyone who will not receive the kingdom of God like a little child will never enter it."

[12] My path has led me to believe that the "Kingdom of Heaven is within." In that, once we awaken to the fact that we're creating our reality and we chose to create in love, we also awaken within us a Christlike Consciousness. The melding of our awareness with Christlike Consciousness is what allows us to enjoy our human experience in various ways. First, we are blessed with awareness of the miracles we experience as we heal. Next, we see the unfolding of the life we're meant to have – a life beyond our wildest dreams.

What castle/life do we want to build? Before realizing our powers as builders, do we create situations that leave us in angst/anger/sadness, etc? Do we not realize said reality is as illusory as the sandcastle on the shore that can disappear with one wave? Poof!

We ARE the child. We shape ALL of our realities and have the power to shift in between them via the subtle frequencies in our emotions. And, we ARE the wave; we have the power to change our outlook and our life. We are in control of our lives. I am in control of my life.

This sense of power and relief washes over me.

I sit in silent meditation.

After several hours, the ceremony concludes and the guides, along with half of the Ayahuasca participants, make their way to the dining area. The other half of the group remains in the temple, slowly awakening from the effects of the medicine, enjoying the quiet time.

The volunteers have prepared a warm and delicious vegetable soup for us. And, after a long night of soul searching, mama bear is hungry.

After three bowls of the soup, I'm full and decide to head to my cabin to rest.

Although there are some lights at the entrance to the trail that leads to the cabin, the darkness is consuming. I enter the canopied trail and get struck by the urge to throw-up. I quickly search for a tree, bush, or shrub to purge. I'm in shock that my body decided to puke *after* the ceremony. What does this mean?

Nicholas seems to appear out of nowhere and puts his left arm around me and escorts me back to the temple to join the handful of participants that remain there. Mid-walk he shares that sometimes the soup has a way of triggering the medicine. As I lay down on my mat he says, "Come out when you're ready. (dramatic pause) You'll know when you're ready."

Talk about setting the tone of what's to come.

I curl up in fetal position and begin to see flashes of my life once again. However, this time, it's completely different. This time, the flashes are illusory; they're images of experiences that haven't happened. Totally imaginary.

I ask myself, "why?" As in, why am I imagining these things. I receive the answer in the form of thoughts. Or, what I like to call "thought drops." Best way I can describe the feeling is this...I feel as if my inner self is connecting with me and I'm translating the vibration into words. And the words continue...Although I've been blessed with awakening to the power of being a deliberate creator of my reality, I'm also here to honor my human experience. How? By having the awareness to feel/see the healing of my relationships right before my eyes.

My thoughts return to the scenes being played out....I'm speaking with, hugging and crying with the folks who've been instrumental in the shaping of the reality from which I'm healing. One by one I start feeling and seeing them heal before my eyes. In one scene, I saw one of the significant males in my life as a small child, alone, frightened and crying. I felt his fear. This scene helped me understand how easy it was for him as a child to build an emotional wall after experiencing much rejection. Also, I now have clarity as to my vibrational set point at the time I attracted him into my reality. I immediately felt one with him, that scene resonated within me; I've been there before, many times – afraid to allow love in. I now see him as an adult, and I energetically extend love and forgiveness to the both of us. We laugh and hug. I feel warmth in my chest and an overwhelming sense of love. I wish him peace. We've healed.

Again and again, I am blessed with visions and feelings surrounding the healing of my relationships.

I now fully understand what it means to honor my human experience.

And, this is what Nicholas means by knowing when I'm ready to join the group. I instinctually laugh under my breath, keeping the volume down out of respect for those who remain in the temple.

Now, I'm ready to eat some more soup.

After putting on my customary boots at the entrance of the temple, I enjoy the brisk air as I once again make my way to the dining area. I'm not quite sure how long I've been under this second trance, that's why I jokingly imagine myself as a racoon, foraging through the leftovers in the dining area.

I see that the pot of soup is more than half full. Hooray for mama bear.

As I sit to enjoy my first bowl of soup, Nicholas, the youngest of the guides, approaches me. With as much endearment as earlier, he asks again, "so this was your first experience?" with a mouthful of soup I do my best to say yes. Similar to John, he's surprised that I had these realizations during my first ceremony. He proceeds to tell me that for most participants, it takes 10 to 15 ceremonies to reach my newly acquired state of awareness. He congratulates me for joining the Ayahuasca family. I shed tears of joy and of course tell myself in a British accent "By George, she's got it!"

Throughout the night, and the multiple bowls of vegetable soup, I attract several of the participants to sit next to me. They ask questions about my experience. And, they begin to divulge intimate details of their lives which resonate with me. This just keeps getting better. These conversations allow me to once again to heal. I see myself in them as we talk about emotions that have impeded their expansion. And, more importantly, I have the awareness to extend love and forgiveness.

Hours later, I'm literally nodding off. I grab my cellphone and choose to exit stage left.

I tell myself, let's try this again. Although darkness was present, my path is lit. Perhaps not literally, but figuratively and in more ways than one. I'm able to make my way to the cabin while enjoying the cool breeze and a burst of energy that has me almost skipping to the cabin.

What a night.

I am wide-awake and excited to journal; I want to capture as much of the experience as possible. Like a scientist going over the results of her experiment, I studiously jot down copious notes. In my mind, I'm gathering all sorts of data that's going to serve as amazing anecdotal evidence for those who read about my journey. Just call me a Spiritual Scientist. My inner child jumps for joy at the thought of the role play.

I say loud enough for my ears only, "Where's my white lab coat?" I laugh. This time loud enough for the sound to fill the cabin.

I look around and notice that the dawn is approaching. Despite my renewed energy, I decided to lay in bed. I want to rest for a few hours before the long road trip home.

The rain outside is soothing and meditative. I hear the drops landing on the roof of the cabin. Then, my attention is drawn to the sound of the raindrops landing on the palm fronds just outside the cabin. I wonder, where are the small reptiles taking shelter? Where are the birds sleeping? And then I smiled at the joy of finding out; finding clarity in all matters is a joy of mine; I revel at the thought of acquiring knowledge. The rain begins demands my attention. The barrage of raindrops resonated inside the cabin. I am once again immersed in the present moment. Purity, that's a word that pops into my mind. I imagine the rain washing away all that's been released tonight, bringing us one step closer to our divine nature.

I drift into a peaceful sleep.

I'm awakened by the sun which is pouring into the cabin. It's relatively early, perhaps I slept 4 hours. No way to tell since the phone is sans charge. At this point, I'm just following my biorhythms. I used the sun as my alarm clock and gingerly packed and got myself together for the drive home.

Before heading out, I decide to stop by the dining area. I walk in and see a healthy continental breakfast laid out for the participants. After enjoying the light meal and surprisingly light conversation, I decide that it's time to get on the road.

Of course, all I can think about is calling Malik to share what I've just experienced. Aaaaand, I remember that the phone needs to be charged, I can't even power it up. Silver lining, I'll plug it in and have more time to digest this experience.

I am immersed in a feeling of appreciation for the spiritual growth and the energetic shift I've undergone this weekend. This time, I'm the one who's surprised. Because I don't shed tears. Simply put, I feel amazing.

Ruby is cruising along the dirt road, yearning to find the smooth asphalt that's going to take her home to Dania Beach.

After this weekend, the word beach will always remind me of the simplicity behind this existence. Yet, the paradox is that it takes complete surrendering to accept. And this thing called surrendering can prove to be difficult for many.

Perhaps the path of most allowance for some is to imagine themselves living life with youthful exuberance.

For the few who can easily take leaps of faith, allow yourself the luxury of surrendering the old reality (created in fear) in order to allow the one created in love in. One where you accept your power to shape those grains of sand into the castles of your dreams.

Beach, grains of sand, castles…my thoughts start to drift to home, and the amazing life I live.

Living in Dania Beach, the Atlantic Ocean is in my backyard. I find a sense of energetic rejuvenation visiting the local beach. Including seeing the young children playing creatively with the sand. Given that I've been an active mother, I especially find joy when I see parents engaging in imaginative play with their children.

The love they're exchanging in that present moment is what yields future experiences that are a reflection of that love.

Little do they know that they are building castles in the sand, in more ways than one.

And the sunrises, I find they are beyond compare. Perhaps I love our sunrises because I emotionally connect with sitting on the empty, wooden lifeguard station off of Perry Street, feeling the emotions I was experiencing at the time, and knowing that I've released those emotions inspires a deep sense of appreciation. I guess that's why I recall the dates of certain sunrises I've witnessed on the beach. Including November 4, 2019, the sunrise on which I met Malik. And, June 23rd, 2020, our first sunrise as lovers. Now *that* story is for another day.

Speaking of Malik, where's my phone?

Chapter Six

THE MAD HATTER IS THE MAGICIAN

By the time I met with Psilocybin in June of 2023, I had already undergone a significant amount of spiritual work. With this new substance, I received a message that would stay with me for a long time: "The Mad Hatter is the Magician," because he realizes that everything is going on inside his head. This seemingly whimsical and paradoxical insight resonated deeply with me. In that moment, I recognized that the external world is merely a reflection of my inner reality. The Magician, or the true creator, is someone who understands that perception is shaped from within.

I had the epiphany that the Mad Hatter was, in essence, having a tea party in his own mind—and the guests at the table were all aspects of himself. Each character was a reflection, a fragmented voice of his psyche playing out in narrative form. The madness, it seemed, was not in the world, but in the illusion of separation that our minds often create. This revelation felt like a profound key to unlocking my own creative potential, and with it, the realization that I, too, was the Magician, shaping the world around me by the power of my thoughts and intentions.

Both Ayahuasca and Psilocybin guided me in unique ways,

revealing layers of my consciousness and opening doors to deeper realms of understanding. Each journey was different, yet they both offered me an opportunity to confront my perceived limitations, shed the old programming, and embrace a new, expansive view of reality. These experiences, though challenging at times, have become integral to my spiritual evolution, serving both as catalysts and companions in my quest to embody my true power as a creator.

The continued use of Ayahuasca and Psilocybin became transformative catalysts, propelling me to make bold and necessary changes in my life. The most significant shift came in January 2024 when I decided to leave my position as an administrator at a mental health facility. Though the role had once felt aligned with my purpose, it had begun to feel constricting and emotionally draining. The work no longer resonated with my evolving consciousness. I realized that I could no longer serve others in the way I wanted while remaining in a space that wasn't aligned with my soul's calling. Leaving that position opened up space for me to pursue a new path—one that felt aligned with my spiritual journey.

After resigning in January of 2024, I felt a sense of freedom—but also an immense weight. I had stepped away from one chapter of my life, yet I found myself plunged into an intense process of transmutation. While I pursued spiritual courses and deepened my studies, I also confronted some of the darkest emotions I had ever faced.

There were days that I contemplated ending it all. The whispers of self-destruction were relentless, like an echo of pain that had been waiting for its moment to surface. At times, the voices felt like they weren't mine, yet they carried the weight of every wound I had ever endured. It wasn't just about what I had left behind in my career—it was about everything I had yet to release within myself.

Then came February 2, 2024. In an Ayahuasca ceremony, I received a message that repeated itself with unwavering clarity: The answer is found within. It was not some grand revelation, nor was it a promise of immediate relief—it was an invitation. An invitation to sit with my pain, to stop running from it, and to surrender to the depths of my own healing.

In the months that followed, I committed myself fully to this journey. Instead of resisting the darkness, I allowed myself to move through it. I deepened my spiritual coursework, exploring teachings that resonated with my soul. I let go of who I thought I had to be and embraced the process of becoming. The pain did not disappear overnight, but I was no longer trapped in it. I was learning to transmute—alchemy in its purest form.

Before my Ayahuasca experience, I delved into Access Bars, a modality that I had been drawn to intuitively after completing a Rolfing[13] series. My Rolfing practitioner, who was also an Access Bars instructor, introduced me to this practice, and I felt an immediate pull to explore it. (Later on, I will also explain how choosing to take an Access Bars course trumped another Ayahuasca experience in November of 2023—and how the decision impacted my relationship with a friend.)

Access Bars is an energy healing technique that involves gently touching 32 points on the head, each linked to different aspects of life—money, control, creativity, healing, and more. These points store thoughts, beliefs, emotions, and patterns that may be limiting us, much like files on a cluttered computer drive that slow down the processing time. By activating them, the accumulated energy releases, making space for clarity, ease, and greater possibilities.

For me, Access Bars became a way to clear the mental clutter that had been weighing me down. Each session felt like peeling back layers of old programming—doubts, fears, traumas—some of which I had not realized I was carrying. It wasn't an instant transformation, but with each session, I felt lighter. My mind, which had often felt like a storm of overanalyzing and intrusive thoughts, began to settle into more peace.

More importantly, Access Bars helped me release emotions I had

---

[13] Add what is Rolfing…more detail to follow

suppressed for years. Memories surfaced, not to torment me, but to be acknowledged and let go. I cried, I laughed, and at times, I simply felt a profound sense of stillness—something I had long been searching for.

Looking back, I see how Access Bars prepared me for the deep inner work that Ayahuasca would later facilitate. It softened the edges of my resistance and opened my heart to surrender, which would be crucial in the transformative months ahead.

Next, I took a few courses in mediumship. It was after my second course in mediumship, a pivotal point in my spiritual evolution, that I had a profound epiphany about the continuation of transmuting deep-seated emotions—specifically guilt and shame. These feelings had been lingering beneath the surface for so long, and I had not fully realized how much they had been holding me back. The Monday morning following the second course, and after ingesting a dose of Psilocybin combined with THC, I experienced a profound breakthrough.

Chapter Seven

THE VOICE, ALAN WATTS, AND THE ROACHES

It's the evening of Monday, April 22nd 2024.

The last few days have been transformative. I feel open. I thought I was going to say that I felt open to *something*. Then my brain caught up to my heart and I stopped typing.

I had to sit with the feeling. I realized that my heart was feeling more than it had in a long while; I felt open. I immediately felt an overflow of love and joy. My mind was also in a state of bliss because of the experiences leading up to the telling of this story. I was able to connect dots to reveal a bigger picture for me to ponder. I was in a state of awe and appreciation. There was balance between emotion and logic.

My fingers stopped typing.

I decided to enjoy those feelings for a bit. Little did I know that I would have more to add, based on what happened the following day, Tuesday, April 23rd, 2024.

I resumed writing Wednesday, April 24th, 2024. As a result, the story has two parts. Part 1 is comprised of what happened before I started writing the evening of Monday the 22nd. Part 2 is about what happened after the 23rd.

Let's begin.

Part I.
It's the morning of Monday, April 22, 2024

After a weekend of channeling and remote viewing I felt emotionally tired. I did find this interesting. What was I doing that was creating the tiredness? Was it my approach? My mindset? A belief system? I knew the answer would be revealed at the appropriate time.[14]

Let's take it to the beginning - Johanne Rutledge's Alpha Two class, which started Saturday, April 20th. Alpha Two is a 2-day mediumship course. Being that Alpha One is a prerequisite course, Alpha Two gave me access to additional tools on how to interact with energy. For example, that Saturday, I learned to remote view. Perhaps you're wondering, what is remote viewing[15]? The best way to explain it is using your mind to see a distant or unseen subject. The goal is to provide information about a person, an event, location or object that is hidden from physical view and separated by distance.

In this case, we were taught to remote view with the purpose of clearing a home of entities.

The experience was amazing! We started by entering an Alpha state, which is done with a series of breathing exercises. For the students it also included creating a protective energetic bubble. Once in the Alpha state, I travel with my mind's eye to my spiritual workshop. The workshop is an energetic space I created full of spiritual tools to work with. Among them, portals that allowed me to roam freely and explore other dimensions. In essence, it's the "permission slip" I've given myself to free my mind.

Once in Alpha state, I allowed myself to feel sensitive to Sarah's energy. I felt a passing wave of sadness. What came next was an intense feeling of grief that brought me to tears. I asked Sarah if she suffered

---

[14] On that day, the answer didn't come. What I did receive, were several eye-opening epiphanies which are mostly documented here.

[15] The term "remote viewing" was coined by physicist Russel Targ and Harold Puthoff, who were parapsychology researchers at Stanford Research Institute (SRI). They coined the term to distinguish remote viewing from the related concept of clairvoyance.

from depression. She mentioned that she's experienced depression for many years and has been feeling better. I channeled love to her.

Sarah provided the street address of her boyfriend's two-bedroom apartment. I began to see the streets of Fort Lauderdale. I saw an apartment building and then saw myself gliding through a hall just before I reached her boyfriend's apartment door. I felt the doorknob in my hand, and I turned it to open the door. What actually happened is that I found myself reappearing on the other side of the door, i.e. inside the apartment.

I immediately felt a warm sensation on my forehead (in between my eyebrows) while I'm receiving the results of the energy scan of the apartment. I felt entities present. My goosebumps and chills are my version of Spidey senses. Trust that they were tingling.

As mentioned before, this was my first remote viewing experience. Imagine the excitement of giving an accurate description of the apartment.

As you walk into the apartment you can find the kitchen to the left. Followed by dining area sans furniture followed by a living area that ends with glass sliding doors. I didn't sense any dense entities in the common areas.

The two bedrooms were split by the living area. The bedroom on the left had the bath inside the room. It also had a walk-in closet. I felt this room pushing me away. According to Sarah, this room "was the worst."

The bedroom to the right shares the bath in the common area, by way of a connecting door.

I chose to enter the bedroom on the right.

Upon entering the bedroom, I saw a small round table at the far end of the room, just in front of the large window. The table was covered by a white tablecloth with a laced trim. Sitting at the table was a couple, dressed in English-styled, turn of the century, clothing. They were casually having a cup of tea.

I thanked them for their presence and purpose served. I asked them to leave the apartment. They immediately disappeared. The room felt clear. Sarah shared this was her boyfriend's room and that she had cleared it several times.

It was now time to enter the hotspot, the second bedroom. According to Sarah, ever since she started frequenting the apartment, the roommate has been bothered by entities that make noises at night. The noises are loud enough to keep the roommate up at all hours of the night.

When I first entered the second bedroom, I saw the bed on the wall opposite the door. I asked Sarah for confirmation. She laughed. Apparently, she'd remote viewed into the bedroom and that's where she also sees the bed. In actuality, the physical headboard is against the wall alongside the door we used to enter the room.

Upon entering, I felt a wave of emotions, very similar to the sadness and grief I felt when I connected with Sarah. This time the sadness and grief were in the form of human-shaped dark shadows without faces. They were flying and darting across the room. Tears ran from my eyes, my way of acknowledging them. I also sensed fear; they were afraid of me.

Within seconds of wiping my tears, the shadowy entities stopped flying around the room and gathered, squatting side-by-side on the floor in the far-right corner of the room. The longer I stared at the corner, my sight became keener. I was able to see a small crack that was emitting a bright light. I shared this observation with Sarah. She told me that there used to be a portal located there and she sealed it a while back.

A sixth sense took over and knew what had to be done.

I thanked the shadows of sadness and grief for the purpose they served and asked them to depart by way of that small crack in the corner. When the last of them left I began to close the portal. I felt like Dr. Strange, it was surreal. I felt myself smiling ear to ear while my hands made circular motions. My palms were also emitting a light that was sealing the portal.

I made my way to the closet.

Deep breath.

The closet was full of entities, many dark shadows. They began hissing at me. The shadows would take turns morphing into the shape of a mouth full of sharp teeth (think of the Marvel character Venom). This mouth would lead the group by approaching the door of the closet and it would hiss above all the other shadowy entities. Often times, they would collaborate by joining up to make the shape of a much larger mouth that also hissed above others.

I felt their anger. They were upset at my presence. Shortly thereafter I felt their anger melt away into fear.

I found it amazing that I was able to feel them. After immediately feeling comfortable with the new sensations, all I felt was love for them.

I wasn't afraid.

I wasn't casting out "demons," per se. I felt I was casting out anger, grief and guilt. And for many, these emotions can be considered "demons." "Demons" that lead them to do or say things that later create other "demons." Often, one of the names we give them is regret.

While I felt these emotions, they quickly turned to pity. Then with the wand of empowerment, I saw myself recognizing the value they must have served. I felt encouraged to thank them before deciding that I was going to ask them to leave.

The warmth I felt in my chest made it evident to me that I was channeling love. I found it fascinating that without me vocalizing, the slump-shouldered shadows lined up single-file. Their walk of shame led them to the connecting bathroom. One at a time they jumped, feet-first, into the toilet. I'm chuckling as I tell Sarah, "They are literally jumping into the toilet[16]."

This is how I spent my Saturday.

Let's return to the morning of Monday, April 22nd, 2024.

Now that I have recapped the weekend, I decided to move on to

---

[16] The importance of the toilet. Later in Part I you'll find out how a toilet triggered a chain of events. A series of dots that were connected. The result was me giving a watery send-off to some of the shadows in my closet. The repressed emotions that were also deserving of love.)

the matter at hand. I was pondering, go into the office or stay at home?

After a brief pause and a deep breath, I made my decision. The last thing on my mind was stepping into an environment where I would be surrounded by the unsettled energy of dozens who've been dealing with schizophrenia for decades. Speaking of schizophrenia, I've always felt that it's a misunderstood diagnosis. My take on the matter is that the veil is thinner for some more than others. They've been hearing "the voices (entities) in their head" for years. Only to end up numb from the anti-psychotic meds. I'm not knocking Western medicine. Just saying that based on my experience, I look forward to an alternative approach. Back to the story...

The decision to stay home was easy to make. I craved time for myself. And I wanted to allow myself the time to process the events of the weekend. I didn't have a plan of any sort. I knew the goal – alone time to reflect.

I did something I hadn't done in a few months. I waited until the coast was clear (i.e. till I was alone) at home and partook in mushrooms. Not a large dose. I took 1.5 grams of psilocybin. To give you an idea, that's more than a microdose, which is around 0.25 grams and, nowhere near the 5.0 gram Terrence McKenna[17] "Hero's Dose." I'd say I took a light-to-medium dose.

When the psilocybin kicks in, the present moment awareness turns up a few notches. Interestingly enough, the awareness assumes a voice. It proceeds to state the obvious plus provide perspective. For example, it describes what I'm doing or I've done and gives commentary that assists me in connecting the dots of micro matters so that I can have a macro "aha" moment.

Today's gift is the awareness of the deep-seated guilt and regret I have felt and then later repressed in the past couple of decades. Another gift is the sight of past experiences with another perspective. And, the

---

[17] Terrence Kemp McKenna (11/16/1946-4/3/2000) was an ethnobotanist and mystic who advocated for the responsible use of naturally occurring psychedelic plants.

interesting twist is that I received a bonus epiphany. that my relationship with marijuana was being influenced by the degree of guilt.

Let me set the scene. I hope to help *you* connect the dots.

Well, I've already set the stage for you. You already know that I'm under the influence of mushrooms.

While under the FULL influence of the psylocibin, my buddy Bob[18] decides to call me to talk.

Backstory on Bob – We've known one another for almost 30 years. We met while working in the same claims department of an insurance company. And then, our paths continued to cross at various other companies for several years.

It wasn't until 2011 that we became close friends. Although I'm 10 years younger than him I would say that I often play the role of Bob's older sister. I feel that I'm the older sister he's never had. He comes from an Italian and devoutly Catholic family of 8 kids, comprised of 6 boys and 2 girls. If I recall correctly, there are a pair of twins in there. Bob would describe his father as a mean son of a bitch and his mother as subservient. His father was former military and his mother a devout housewife a la 1950s.

He's shared with me how much he appreciates my viewpoint. He's described it as feminine, strong and intelligent. He approaches me to discuss several topics, including spiritual matters. Also, after many years of knowing one another, Bob has been a witness to my evolution and appreciates that I can understand various perspectives. Even though I often shared my thoughts when they were solicited, I always reminded Bob that the answer was always within *him*.

Continuing…Bob has an interesting habit of spending a lot of time in the closet, literally. He loves to FaceTime me while sitting naked on a stool in the closet.

When he first started doing this, I thought he was a pervert who had the hots for me. After almost 30 years of friendship, these days I feel he suppresses his sexuality due to guilt and fear of judgment.

---

[18] Name has been changed.

Perhaps the reason behind his affinity with spending time "in the closet."

Bob has a way of coming in and out of my life. For the last 4 months Bob and I have been speaking several times a week.

He's been on a journey of self-love. He started seeing a therapist. He journals. He reads the Louise Hay's books I gave him. He's learning to meditate. He's allowing himself to feel and cry. He's starting to figure out who the "real" Bob is.

I respect his process and keep my feelings about his sexuality to myself. For now.

Enough backstory and now back to *the* story.

Today, after being in conversation with Bob for a few minutes, I decided to roll a blunt.

Bob is excited that I am going to smoke. According to him, it's not often that he sees me "be human."

As mentioned before, for the last few months, I've been his listening ear. He's made me his Jiminy Cricket of sorts. An alternative voice to the Catholic mass he and his family hears on Sundays. Since I offer him zero judgment, he loves to talk while I listen. In fact, today, he "confessed" that he's frequented many gay bars. I say "confessed" because in the same breath he said he wouldn't want his wife to know. My spidey senses felt the guilt. He's slowly coming out of the closet, in more ways than one. I found it interesting that today he was hanging out in his wife's closet.

News of my decision has him so giddy that he decides to join me for a smoke-break. to step out of the closet during our conversation to join me for a smoke-break.

Since we're on FaceTime I see Bob walking around to make sure he has the all-clear. In other words, he wants to make sure that his wife isn't home to "catch him the act of smoking." As such, he's developed a tendency to be hypervigilant before partaking in anything he considers naughty, or out of line.

Bob doesn't roll joints or blunts; he's a pipe smoker. He breaks down some flower, puts it in his pipe and walks to the bathroom. The screen goes dark. Then, he turns on the light and I'm reminded of Bob's preference for nudity. Bob is butt-ass naked, straddling the open toilet with the pipe in one hand a lighter in the other.

We light up and proceed to have some small talk for the first few minutes. Thus, allowing the smoking experience to set in.

Having the psylocibin in full effect allowed the THC to come in with such smoothness that I felt an immediate sense of enhanced awareness coupled with a relaxation that released my tight grip on overthinking.

In Bob's case, he often becomes very talkative while under the influence of many substances. Today he felt inspired to ask me about my history with marijuana. He wanted to know how I got started, why I smoked, and about my smoking habits.

I felt THE voice breaking the 4th wall and start to respond for me. I went on to share with Bob that I didn't care for the lingering smell of the marijuana nor do I enjoy it's a suppression of my energy. I've come to appreciate my Energizer Bunny-type energy.

After stating this, Bob went on and on about a subject that till today I cannot recall. I couldn't hear him because THE voice was busy asking me a series of questions, starting with "what does Bob represent in your story Denise?" Followed by, "why is Bob smoking over the toilet?" I could sense that the introspection session was about to start.

I decided to end the conversation with Bob. I told him that I had to sit with myself for a bit in order to process my emotions.

On the surface he said okay and agreed to reconnect another time. Regardless of the words that came out of his mouth, I felt resistance.

Bob was like a little boy in love with his mother, who feels he's being "abandoned" by her at kindergarten on the first day of school. That was the kind of resistance I felt.

I had to metaphorically pry him off and subconsciously tell him that it was going to be okay. He acquiesced.

Afterwards, THE voice and I started to have a heartfelt conversation about the last 12 years of my life, including the 12-year relationship I've had with marijuana.

Alchemic Healings

Backstory…I've been hanging out with marijuana for the last 12 years. 5 years prior to that, it would poke its head in the scene to say hello. Before that we're talking crickets.

In 2023, I had an adversarial relationship with her. And during that time, I read Graham Hancock's essay "Getting Rid of the Green Bitch." I admit, I felt quiet validation knowing Graham nicknamed her The Green Bitch. At the time, the given name validated the anger that stemmed from listening to internal dialogue that was loud and often self-deprecating when I was in her company.

Picture this and perhaps you'll understand. Here's the visual of a cycle I was caught in. It starts with an image of me having an aha moment that includes me cutting back or eliminating marijuana. Followed by me smoking and finding a self-deprecating internal dialogue yelling at me "why can't I get this bitch's claws out of me?" That internal voice would continue to punish and berate me for crossing the boundary *I* had set.

And now here it is Monday, April 22nd of 2024 and I'm speaking with THE voice while Bob is straddling the toilet, asking many questions about my smoking habits. I also had a fleeting mental image of the entities jumping in the toilet over the weekend.

I told myself, I'm beginning to understand my relationship with marijuana.

She's typically stirred up emotions that lurked deep inside of me. On the surface, the emotions would disguise themselves as negative patterns/behaviors. In my case, I would typically smoke 5 to 6 blunts a day. I would occasionally cut it out for weeks or months at a time. Only to find my way back to it. I would introduce the MJ slowly; the reboot would often include nursing a blunt for 2 days. Then I would start the one blunt-a-day stage. Lastly, it would go back to several blunts a day. The long-standing effect of the constant infusion of THC was such that despite all the epiphanies, I would remain stagnant throughout the day. In other words, I would possess all these inspired yet fleeting ideas and rarely did anything with them. I'd feel regret followed by guilt.

Today, I allowed myself to get into my feels and promised that I would document the journey. I opened the door to the long-standing guilt and stagnant energy to be transmuted for a higher purpose.

I felt a tinge of it. Where was the guilt coming from? As mentioned earlier, I had been smoking for 12 years. What also happened 12 years ago? My divorce from Andrew, the father of my two amazing daughters.

I don't regret the divorce. What I've come to understand is that the way I went about uncoupling could've been handled differently. I could sense that this is where the guilt was coming from.

THE voice was helping me feel the trail of heartache I had left behind. The introspection started with Andrew and ended with my daughters. I finally felt the guilt and grief that I'd kept in the closet for 12 years. They were now hissing at me. I cried for what felt like hours. I allowed my tears to flow, recognizing that I was ushering the dark emotions out of the recesses of my soul and into the light so that they could be showered with love. And, in doing so, I let myself know that they no longer needed to be a part of my experience.

They walked out of the proverbial closet. Now, I felt an impulse to flush the marijuana in my possession down the toilet.

Backstory…I had been smoking for the past 3 weeks after a 2-month hiatus. To my surprise, when I decided to start smoking again, I received over a pound of marijuana from a close friend. By the time I made the decision to flush the stash down the toilet, I was down to about an ounce. No, I didn't smoke almost a pound in 3 weeks. I knew that I didn't want to keep a pound of it around me. At the time, felt it would've been too tempting, especially since I was telling myself that the long-term goal was to quit. I packaged it into small bags and started making rounds. I gave the same way I received, for free.

Looking back, I'm now making connections between the folks I gave the bud to and what emotions they represent in my life. There's always a connection. Those stories are for another time.

What remained in my possession was approximately an ounce and it was packaged in quarters.

As I held each quarter, I chose who I would focus my energy on. The first quarter was dedicated to Mark, my most recent ex-husband.

The second and third quarters were dedicated to my daughters. The last quarter was dedicated to Andrew.

I was inspired to hold the respective quarters in both hands while I thought of the person. I would then forgive myself and them for all perceived transgressions on either side. I would hold onto the bud and cry. That was my form of release. I'd also remain closed-eyed and silent until the thought of the person inspired joy instead of guilt or sadness. Once I reached joy, I'd flush the bud down the toilet.

Since I had to gradually flush Andrew's I decided to meditate for a few minutes. The few minutes turned into an hour. After the intense emotional release, the meditation turned into a nap.

Later that evening, Malik walked into the room and awakened me from my slumber with tender kisses.

As I rubbed my eyes, he reminded me that I hadn't finished flushing the bud (i.e. Andrew's quarter). I walked into the bathroom and found what looked like a dark green portal instead of the loo. Once fully awake, I quickly caught onto the reality in front of me; the toilet was full of wet marijuana, there was what looked like chunky dried oregano sprinkled across the floor, plus, there was a partially full packet of bud next to the sink.

By now I was sober. I decided to wrap it up quickly. I wasn't thinking more about Andrew. In my mind, I just wanted to clean up the mess.

Afterwards, I enjoyed the rest of the evening with Malik. I especially loved attempting to explain what transpired. I cut the explanation short and explained that I was going to write about it.

Part II

Tuesday, April 23rd, 2024. Day two of epiphanies...Alan Watts and the roaches.[19]

Like a toddler who was learning to walk, I found myself enthused

---

[19] The word roaches is NOT being used to refer to the insect. Roaches here means the remnants of a blunt (or joint) after most of it has been smoked.

to start the day yet still figuring out the next step. I was once again establishing a new routine that didn't include smoking. In my mind, gone were the days of waking and baking. Instead of twiddling my thumbs, I decided to jump into something.

What did I do? I cleaned. I had my reasons.

Here's my take on the matter. I'm learning to appreciate the meditative space that cleaning can provide. Not only am I enjoying the result of creating a clean environment, the cleaning in and of itself has become a form of meditation.

I had my Beats headphones in, listening to Billy Carson's 432Hz Merkabah Meditation on a loop.

I started with a deep cleaning of the kitchen.

Before my YouTube premium subscription, occasionally ads would play before the meditation would re-start. On this morning, the first ad began with a young Alan Watts speaking about reality and consciousness. I've come to enjoy listening to Alan Watts. I find the sound of his voice soothing, plus I resonate with the messages he delivers.

My next thought was that Andrew had introduced me to Alan Watts.

It may help to provide a brief backstory on Andrew. I mentioned him in Part I. You may recall that he's the father of my two girls.

He and I were both raised Jehovah's Witnesses (JW) and were accustomed to a very restrictive upbringing. We met through one of my sisters. We had a 6-month "courtship." Then married.

Shortly after we exchanged nuptials, we decided to leave the JW organization. This was HUGE. Walking away implied that you were drawing a line in the sand between doing what your heart desired and the organization's restrictive belief system. It also meant being ostracized by all of the JWs you knew. After years of shouldering the weight the of all the rules, you can only imagine what it felt like to just drop it all and walk away. Think of a spring being held down tight then having the pressure released. These two springs flew ALL over the place!

Suffice to say that the 15 years of marriage are full of many stories. One day, I will share many of them.

Back to Andrew and Alan Watts. In making the connection that I first learned of Alan Watts through Andrew, I wasn't thinking about Andrew the father or Andrew the husband. I thought about the 26-years young Andrew. The Andrew I married. He was full of hope, searching for meaning and spiritual truth. He was on a spiritual quest. He was a big fan of Alan Watts and Zen Buddhism. He found joy in his guitar, yoga and reading. He worked and pretty much kept to himself. He did his best to introduce me to this "new" world he'd been creating, so different from the JW world that we had been a part of. Today it sunk in that my wounds at the time didn't allow me to accept his invitation.

As if on of queue, Malik walks into the kitchen to say goodbye. What's the importance of this synchronicity? In my eyes and in my life, Malik is a picture of the Divine Masculine. He is kind, loving, tender, intelligent, spiritual and possesses an emotional intelligence that is off the charts. I'm forever thankful and appreciative for having him in my life. The love we've exchanged has catapulted me into a realm where my spiritual evolution has been moving upward and onward at warp speed.

Suffice to say, he walks in and proceeds to embrace me. Although he is not privy to the internal dialogue that I've been having, he senses the disturbance in the force. I feel his love wash over me with such warmth and tenderness that I am compelled to break down into tears. He instinctually knew to hold me in his arms and hold emotionally present space for me while I let out deep guttural cries. He encouraged me to take deep breaths.

At that time, I felt I needed time to figure out the emotions behind my tears. I had a clue what the tears were about and wanted to sit with these emotions for a while. I wasn't up for discussing my feelings. While the side of my wet face was on his tear-stained shirt, I mumbled, "I'm processing." He said all that he intended to say by holding me tighter and kissing my forehead. He asked no further questions at this time. His unconditional love for me always allows him to "let me be." He knows that after I sit with the experiences, I typically do one of two things – one, verbally relay the details of my epiphanies or two, excitedly ask him to read what I've written about the epiphanies.

He looks at me deeply in my eyes and tells me he loves me. He kisses me on my lips and gifts me another kiss on the forehead for good measure.

I hugged him again and told him how much I looked forward to seeing him later this afternoon.

I walked him to the edge of the stairs and wished him an amazing day.

Like a small child, I ran inside and to the back sliding glass so that I could observe his car departing. When he drove off, I waited around for about 5 minutes before I started searching for the roaches.

Side note: I just realized that I haven't shared something material. Today, I took some more mushrooms. This time, about 2 grams.

THE voice was present. And, of course, it was adding its two cents about my actions. You see, I was being very generic and kind to myself when I said that that I was searching for roaches. What I was doing was scavenging for them. By definition, scavenging implies that I was searching for and collecting items from discarded waste. Well, that's exactly what I did. Imagine this, I'm on my hands and knees on the patio, looking for viable roaches through the small piles of roaches that I've compulsively collected. I even went through the trash to get the bright green pack of Grabba leaf I use to roll my blunts. When I found it, I felt like I struck gold!

Meanwhile, THE voice, in an uncondemning fashion, encouraged me to remain a neutral observer of my actions. I started to recall images of me on the patio floor. I thought about the residents I served as an administrator of mental health facilities.

In my observations, those who have been exposed to the long-term use of antipsychotics and antidepressants plus they've been living in facilities for years, are often addicted to nicotine. And the cheapest way to go about satisfying the craving was to smoke filtered cigars. Imagine a filtered cigarette made with a blend of pipe tobacco. They lived off a $54 monthly stipend for personal expenses which they mainly smoked up. Despite the staff constantly discouraging them, some would scavenge through the discarded cigar butts around the large outside patio to see which ones still had a few puffs left. Despite doing my best to remain understanding of their behavior, I must say that at the time I found it kind of gross.

Now, I looked down and saw my dirty fingers. They were dirty from the ash and burnt marijuana that I was separating from the salvageable and smokeable flower in the roaches. These are the same roaches that were acquired while on my hands and knees on an outside patio. My mother came to mind, and I laughed. She always encouraged me to live a life with zero judgment. And right now, her voice was in my head, and she was saying "think about what you criticize, because what you criticize you imitate." I closed my eyes and took a couple of breaths. I gained perspective.

I joyfully pondered the fact that I had gathered enough flower to roll husky blunt. I sat in a dining room chair I placed by the open sliding glass door and lit up.

Minutes later, as the THC kicks in, THE voice reminds me that yesterday, I flushed ALL the fresh bud down the toilet. I was encouraged to sit with the question – what is the reason behind me smoking today? Despite all of yesterday's purging, I felt a tinge of guilt. The cathartic crying while in Malik's arms minutes earlier must've created the gateway for the guilt to crawl out long enough for me to decide that I am going to snatch it up and hug it out and bid it adieu.

A mental image of Alan Watts pops into my head. ANDREW!

As mentioned earlier, when I met Andrew, he was on a spiritual quest, searching for *his* version of truth. Looking back, I see that he continuously invited me to join him, either explicitly or implicitly. He wasn't asking me to join in on his formulating belief system. He was asking me to explore something spiritual, regardless of the path. I can now admit that I had a lot of emotional resistance within me during that time. I wasn't ready to go down a spiritual path.

I was stuck in what I call "the lower chakra world" which consists of imbalances in the lower three chakras – the root, sacral and solar plexus. These imbalances are typified often by a hyper fixation on many things sexual and/or materialistic, among others. I wasn't the exception.

In my case, I led a very healthy sex life as a married woman, often having sex twice a day. I was in my mid-twenties quickly approaching a six-figure income. And, after leaving the JW organization, the last thing I wanted was to engage in anything spiritual. In my mind, that word was synonymous with religion. And religion, to me, was synonymous with restrictions.

Instead of speaking up and sharing these thoughts with Andrew, I kept quiet and held back my feelings. My silence implied consent.

After 10 years of marriage, the emotional dam broke. I started going against the proverbial grain. I made a series of surprising choices that befuddled many people. The summation of the choices resulted in, what I felt, was a clusterfuck. I knew I was going to land on my feet. I always did. The how? I was clueless. I was also oblivious to the notion that I had desensitized myself to the trail of heartache I left behind. It was just yesterday that I pealed the layers on that onion named guilt. By the looks of it, some remained.

The tears that flowed allowed me to feel the guilt that I had been carrying as it related to Andrew. I forgave myself for creating a reality that took him away from his path. At least the versions of himself I chose to interact with.

Yes, everyone has their journey. Nonetheless, I am a firm believer that people are going to give you whatever version of themselves you expect. It's resonance.

And, regardless of whether we are aware of it, we are creating those interactions. Especially those in A Course In Miracles (ACIM) calls special relationships.[20] My marriage to Andrew falls under that category – a special relationship.

---

[20] Online source found at awakening2onelove.com provided one of the most concise and precise definitions of the special relationship that I was able to find. According to an online *Healing and Special Relationships* Workshop held on February 18, 2018, it is described as follows: "The special relationship is our ego's feeble substitute for the love of God. His love is always shining within us, but out awareness of it has been blocked by our ego attempts to find it outside of us, in the form of a "special relationship" with another human being."

All I can think of is the line in ACIM, "How can he live, with all your sins upon him? And who must be his conqueror but you?"[21]

As such, for many years I chose to blame him for all our problems, making him the "bad guy." Of course, he delivered.

I came to this awareness circa 2017, when I was a beginner student of ACIM. Even though I understood the concept of forgiving myself the seed of guilt took root. Here we are 12 years after the divorce looking at the fruit that it's created – a direct result of cause and effect. Also, in this case, the fruit appears rotted because I had allowed my guilt to mask itself as anger. Years ago, I felt justified in the infidelity that ultimately led to our divorce.

Again, the words of ACIM remind me of my choice. "The special love relationship is the ego's most boasted gift, and one which has the most appeal to those unwilling to relinquish guilt."

Although there isn't a romantic love, I do love Andrew. I mentioned earlier that I met him by way of one of my sisters. I was twelve years old when we met. That being said, this is a story that as of today, is 36 years in the making.

In some way, I held myself responsible for contributing to his spiritual derailment. And, In the experiences I had been creating for myself, I've been looking at him through the eyes of guilt. In doing so, he is going to behave in a way to "punish" me with behavior that would fuel the anger and my underlying guilt.

For the first time in twelve years, I acknowledged and accepted accountability for what I had contributed to my view of today's version of Andrew.

I saw the cycle I had been caught in. It was a vicious cycle that I was choosing to stop today.

Upon asserting this to myself and to the Universe, I wiped my tears. I took a deep breath, and a wave of tranquility washed over me.

There was a strong urge to reach out to Andrew. Without

---

[21] ACIM Chapter 24, Section I. Specialness as a substitute for love. Subsection 5. Lines 9 and 10.

hesitation, I picked up the phone and I texted Andrew. I said, "I'm sorry for breaking your heart."

I knew I had experienced a shift in my reality. Or, what I like to call a "glitch in the matrix." I knew that my future had been altered.

Whether or not he responded, or what he responded is not what matters. I did what I felt I needed to do as part of forgiving myself. What he chooses to do with the apology I extended is on him now.

What mattered to me I that at this moment I felt the last my shadowy entities squirming about. After years of lurking in the closet, they were ready to receive the love that I was ready to give.

And they took the plunge.

Chapter Eight
ANGELS AT SUNRISE

These entheogens once again opened me to a deeper understanding of the emotions I had carried for so long. Guilt and shame, though painful, revealed themselves as old energy patterns—stagnant water in the body and mind. I began to see that they had been tethered to past beliefs that whispered I was unworthy of joy or freedom. Yet as I sat with these feelings, I realized they were not part of my true essence. They were illusions—dense, learned energies I had the power to transmute into love and acceptance.

With the help of Psilocybin, I saw through the layers of conditioning that shaped how I perceived myself. These emotions were not mine to carry. That simple truth lifted something from my spirit, offering a profound sense of relief and liberation. I began to practice forgiveness—first toward myself, then outward. In doing so, I made space for healing and deeper compassion.

This alchemy shifted how I viewed myself and my relationships. Guilt and shame, once shackles on my soul, now stood as invitations—doorways into deeper light. These revelations strengthened my commitment to living a life of alignment, one rooted in truth, self-love, and peace.

Each modality—Access Bars®, mediumship, and psilocybin—felt like a steppingstone leading me into greater remembrance.

Access Bars® quieted the noise in my mind. Mediumship expanded my awareness of unseen energies. Psilocybin shattered old perceptions. As I integrated all of this, I felt drawn toward Reiki. It didn't feel like just another modality—it felt like a calling. A next step in the integration of everything I was remembering.

It was Malik who first suggested I explore Reiki. A close friend of his was a Reiki master teacher, and through that connection, I was led to one of two Reiki mentors who would guide me. The timing felt divinely orchestrated—as if the universe had been lining things up long before I noticed.

By April, I stepped away once again from alcohol and marijuana. This time, it wasn't about control or deprivation—it was about resonance. I wanted clarity. I wanted to be fully present for what Reiki might reveal. That commitment carried me through the weeks ahead as I deepened my study.

By mid-May, I began my first Reiki course.

For those unfamiliar, Reiki is a form of energy healing that channels universal life force energy through the hands. It works on the principle that energy flows through all living things, and that by restoring balance, we promote healing on physical, emotional, and spiritual levels. I learned to attune myself to this flow—and in doing so, I found a profound connection to my own healing and to the divine energy that moves through us all.

Reiki reminded me that we are all interconnected, and that the energy we send out returns in infinite ways we cannot always see.

Then came May 28, 2024.

I woke before sunrise, feeling a quiet pull to the beach. I had recently completed my Level One certification and was in the middle of my 21-day Reiki self-treatment. That morning felt particularly sacred—as if something unseen had arranged the moment long before I arrived.

I set my chair near the shore and let the sound of the waves soften my mind. Drawn to the water, I waded in up to my knees, letting the ocean cleanse and ground me. When I returned to my chair, I noticed something strange: a second set of footprints next to mine, though I had walked alone. I didn't dwell on it—but it felt like a soft whisper: you are not alone.

I began my self-treatment, placing my hands on my body and entering a state of deep peace. My mind stilled. My heart opened. I surrendered completely.

When I opened my eyes, two women were approaching me—Millie and Becca. Millie was especially radiant and kind. She shared something that left me speechless.

She said that when she passed by earlier, she saw me "hugging myself." A perfect way to describe the posture of Reiki.

And then, she said she had seen angels.

Large, luminous beings with majestic wings surrounding me, cocooning me in divine light. She said the energy around me radiated healing. That it was pure. That I was enveloped in protection and grace.

I cried. Tears of affirmation. Tears of surrender.

For years, I had carried skepticism. After leaving the Jehovah's Witnesses, I had become an agnostic, even an atheist. But this moment—this reflection from a complete stranger—felt like divine confirmation. It cracked something open in me. I was being seen—not just as a person, but as a soul on a sacred journey. Her words were a balm. Her presence, a mirror.

Millie said something I'll never forget: that the skepticism had been necessary to arrive at this depth of knowing. That I was exactly where I needed to be.

That morning became a cornerstone of my Reiki path. A sacred reminder that the healing we offer ourselves becomes a ripple in the greater ocean of life. We may not always see how it touches others—but the energy speaks.

And that day, it spoke through Millie.

That sacred moment opened something deeper. I felt pulled to explore the Akashic Records—an energetic archive of the soul's journey across all lifetimes. Through courses and self-guided sessions, I began receiving insights that helped me understand my purpose, my patterns, and my divine design.

And then something profound happened.

In one course, I confirmed a revelation I had previously glimpsed in a self-guided past life regression: the man who owned the medical group I had recently joined had been my brother in a life 2,000 years ago. In that lifetime, I was a Jewish man who left the religion of my upbringing to follow the teachings of Yeshua. His son—my previous employer at the mental health facilities—had been our father.

This life now mirrored that karmic thread. Both men, Orthodox Jews. Me, a Hispanic woman walking a path of spiritual alchemy. The polarity was striking. And yet, beneath the surface, a divine symmetry.

King Solomon—one of my most trusted guides—helped me integrate these visions. His wisdom echoed in my heart, showing me that these weren't random memories. They were invitations to heal through time. To close loops. To forgive across lifetimes.

Through Reiki, through the Records, through the presence of Solomon—I began to see that healing isn't just for now. It echoes across the ages.

By June, I accepted that my role at the medical practice had been karmically appointed. I had learned what I needed. I had remembered what I came to reclaim.

And just as one chapter was closing, another called to me clearly: Peru.

Chapter Nine

SACRED VALLEY, SACRED VISION

I first became aware of a spiritual retreat in Peru, where they held Ayahuasca ceremonies through a friend I had serendipitously met at a Colombian café.

To truly share the story of my trip to Peru, I feel it's important to explain how I discovered this place. More importantly, I want to share the story of the person who introduced it to me. There was an undeniable energetic connection between us, one that played a significant role in guiding me toward this next step on my journey.

It was a crisp November morning in 2022 when I walked into a small Colombian café near our home in Dania Beach, Florida. The scent of rich coffee was swirling in the air.

That day was no different than any other. I wore my "uniform" which consisted of shorts, a blue jacket that came down to my knees and my favorite pair of cowboy boots (Fat Baby by Ariat). Waffles – my beautiful goldendoodle – was trotting beside me on a leash.

As I approached the counter, I noticed a woman standing there, poised to place her order. Something about her energy caught my attention, but it was the tattoo on her left bicep that truly drew me in – an upside-down triangle, the symbol for water.

As a Pisces, a water sign, I felt an immediate connection to the symbol. It was as if it carried an unspoken message meant just for me.

"Nice tattoo," I said, gesturing toward it.

She turned toward me, a bit surprised by the compliment, and a conversation unfolded effortlessly. Somehow, we quickly landed on the topic of Ayahuasca. She seemed taken aback when I not only recognized the word but shared that I had worked with the medicine multiple times. Her curiosity deepened and she leaned in as she told me about her upcoming trip to Peru. In a matter of weeks, she was set to visit Cusco, nestled in the Sacred Valley, to attend a retreat at a center called Etnikas.

Shortly after our encounter at the café, she reached out to me via text. This time, her message was more personal. She wanted to know if Ayahuasca could help unravel a dependence on alcohol. It was a question I understood too well.

As our conversations continued, our relationship deepened. what began as a chance meeting over coffee soon revealed a profound connection between us – one rooted in shared struggles, self-exploration, and the search for something greater than ourselves. We quickly realized that our journeys, though different in many ways, had striking parallels when it came to self-worth and our relationship with alcohol.

For both of us, alcohol had once been more than just a substance – it had been a coping mechanism, a way to silence the deeper wounds we hadn't yet fully confronted. It wasn't about the drink itself, but rather what it represented: escape, numbing, the illusion of control. As we exchanged stories, it became clear that we had both been on a path of reclaiming our power, of peeking back the layers of conditioning and self-doubt that had kept us trapped in cycles of self-sabotage.

Beyond our shared experiences with alcohol, there was another thread weaving our connection – astrology. She was an Aquarius, and my Mercury is in Aquarius. This added another layer of familiarity between us. She had a natural tendency to overthink things, analyzing and rationalizing every detail before taking a leap. I understood this intimately. My Aquarian Mercury had shaped the way I processed information, often leading me to seek intellectual understanding before allowing myself to feel. In many ways, our friendship became a reflection of this dynamic: learning when to trust, when to surrender, and when to quiet the mind so the heart could finally speak.

This journey, for both of us, wasn't just about breaking free from past patterns – it was about opening our hearts. Ayahuasca wasn't just a medicine for the mind; it was a gateway to deeper self-acceptance, an invitation to feel beyond logic. And while she was preparing to take this journey to Peru, I was continuing my own, peeling back layers of self-protection, learning that true transformation wasn't about thinking our way through healing – it was about feeling our way through it.

As January 2023 approached and her departure for Peru grew closer, we both knew that this was more than just a journey for her. It was an initiation. A profound turning point. A step toward something neither of us could fully articulate but both instinctively understood.

She returned from Peru on January 15, 2023, describing her journey as the most beautiful and profound experience of her life.

In the days that followed, we stayed in touch, sharing stories, insights and plenty of laughter about our ongoing dance with substances. During this time not only was alcohol at play, but I was also still smoking marihuana. We both had chosen to move away from them yet found ourselves returning to them like pacifiers whenever life became overwhelming.

In that spirit of curiosity and exploration, we decided to experience psilocybin together for the first time. On June 2nd 2023, we shared homegrown mushrooms from a friend of hers, lovingly cultivated with care. The strain Albino Penis Envy was on the menu. We tried it in pill form. We opened the capsules and split nearly 8 grams of ground Psilocybin (4 grams each), using a method called 'lemon tech' to potentiate the experience. It was during this first experience that I received the message about the Mad Hatter being the Magician – because he realizes that everything is happening inside his own mind. I also kept repeating, repeatedly, that I finally understood the beauty behind the madness. It was as if I had been given a glimpse into the divine comedy of existence, where perception shapes reality and everything truly is all in your head.

We had planned to take part in Ayahuasca together on November 11, 2023. However, after completing an intense Rolfing ten-series in October, I felt called to take a different path. Instead of returning to Ayahuasca, I immersed myself in a series of Access Consciousness courses, ultimately becoming an Access Bars practitioner. Alongside these, I also explored mediumship, Reiki, and courses on how to access the Akashic records, each of which deepened my spiritual journey in unique ways.

I must share that my decision to cancel our shared Ayahuasca experience created some tension between us, subtly straining the bond we had formed. We didn't speak about it much, but I could feel a quiet distance growing between us.

As expected, time and space did their work, and by June of 2024, something unexpected stirred within me. I woke up with an undeniable pull – an urge to go to Peru and visit the same retreat that she had gone to. It felt like a calling, an invitation from the universe to step deeper into my own journey.

In July 2024, I took my first trip to Peru, visiting the same retreat center that she had been to. The experience was nothing short of life changing. However, the journey didn't end there. I felt an undeniable call to return, and in January of 2025, I made my second pilgrimage to Peru, deepening the lessons and revelations that began during my first trip. What transpired during these two visits became pivotal in my spiritual and personal journey. This journal captures not only the details of both times I traveled to the retreat, but also the heart-opening moments that led me there and transformed me in the process.

What follows in this book shifts into a journal-style reflection—an intimate recounting of the pull I felt toward this sacred land, the synchronicities that guided me there, and the profound revelations I experienced in Peru. It is an intimate recounting of the pull I felt toward this sacred land, the synchronicities that emerged in the days before I left and the profound revelations I received once I arrived in Peru.

Monday, June 17th 2024.

Peru was the first thing on my mind when I woke up. The pull toward that sacred land was undeniable—like something deep inside me had already begun the journey. I told Malik, with a quiet certainty, that I knew I'd be traveling there soon. I didn't have the logistics—no set date, no clear budget, no mapped-out plan. Just a knowing.

From my calculations, the trip would cost around $3,000, and I found myself wondering how it would all come together. Still, the whisper in my spirit was louder than the worry in my mind.

Later that morning at the office, I shared my heart with Sasha. As I spoke of my longing for Peru, she smiled gently and said, "You have to follow your soul's desire." Her words felt like a soft anointing—confirmation of what I already knew. The universe was speaking. This was a soul call. All that remained was for me to trust the unfolding.

Friday, June 21st 2024 at approximately 3am.

I'm nestled beside the bed in a cozy den of pillows and blankets, *The Emerald Tablet* glowing in my lap as my only companion. Insomnia had found me again, and I'd been awake for about an hour, reading—floating somewhere between the mysteries of Thoth and the weight of the night.

I decided to close my eyes and take a few deep breaths. My body began to soften, drifting into that liminal space between sleep and stillness. That's when I heard them—voices, layered and rhythmic, repeating the same phrase:

"Go to Peru."

Over and over, a chant woven in ether. A chorus that would not relent until I acknowledged it.

In my mind, I whispered back, *"I hear you."*

Silence. Immediate. Complete.

The reverence of that quiet told me everything.

I sat in that stillness, digesting what had just transpired. Monday's calling had already set the stage. Peru was no longer a possibility. It was a truth. I was going. Period. End of sentence.

But the question still lingered—*What next?*

I wanted more than feelings. I was ready for coordinates. I whispered into the darkness:

"Show me a sign."

My heart knew I'd be answered.

Sleep began to pull at me again, soft and sweet, and I returned to bed.

Hours later, golden morning rays pierced through the bedroom's blackout curtains. Despite the lack of sleep, I felt energized and ready. Summer had freed my eldest daughter, Katelynn, from school, and she decided to join me for the day.

I had a craving for coffee—Cuban coffee, specifically. But after missing the turn to my usual spot, I pivoted. *Flow,* I reminded myself. I rerouted to Rendezvous Bakery and Bistro in Fort Lauderdale.

We pulled up and Katelynn chose to wait in the car. I opened the heavy door and was immediately enveloped by the scent of fresh-baked bread and delicate pastries. As I approached the counter, the man behind the register turned his head slightly, smirked, and asked:

"Toasted baguette and cappuccino?"

I smiled and nodded. "Pretty impressive," I replied.

After a bit of small talk, he began speaking to me in Spanish, then paused—checking, perhaps, to see if I understood.

"Where are you from? Do you speak Spanish?"

"I do. I was born in Miami. My parents are Cuban. What about you?"

"Lima, Peru."

Mic drop.

Nicholas, unknowingly, delivered the very sign I had asked for just hours before. He was the message.

Peru was calling. Loud and clear.

I thanked him, blessed his weekend, and left the café with joy rising in my chest.

The Universe had spoken. Again.

I smiled and told myself:

"Denise, you know you are going to Peru. Now sit tight and wait for the details."

Monday, June 24th, 2024.

The melodic buzzing of my phone stirred me awake at 5:55 AM. I leaned over and hit snooze. Nine minutes later, the same. Again and again. By the fifth round, I decided to reach out to Alexa and set an alarm for 7:55 AM instead.

Breakfast is at 10. I'm only ten minutes away. I already know what I'm wearing. I have time to do Reiki.

Done deal. That was my logic for sleeping in—and I was sticking to it.

At 7:55, Alexa declared the start of my day. The extra two hours of sleep felt like a gift—I'd gone to bed late and needed the rest. I got up and reached for my go-to gray, extra-large insulated hoodie that hung to my mid-thigh. Warmth cocooned me instantly. Next, my toes. I grabbed a pair of thick, knee-high socks and slid them on.

Ahhh. Now I can officially start the day.

I had a 10 AM breakfast scheduled with my friend Chris. We originally met over a decade ago when I was working in the insurance industry. A few weeks ago, we reconnected at an Honor Flight event where my oldest daughter and I had volunteered.

This morning, we were set to catch up at Grampa's, a cozy local spot in Dania Beach. I grabbed my phone to send a confirmation text. I've developed the habit of greeting people with either "Grand rising" or "Howdy" depending on the vibe. Today, "Howdy" felt right.

As my fingers quickly typed what I *thought* was "Howdy," I glanced down before hitting send.

"Hi Peru."

I froze in childlike awe, my heart doing somersaults. I had *typed* "Howdy"... but the screen clearly read:

Hi Peru.

I took a screenshot and immediately sent it to Malik. Then I closed my eyes, placed a hand over my heart, and took a few deep breaths—savoring the magic of that moment.

I see you, Universe. I hear you.

Later that evening, I received a commission check in the mail. The amount was **exactly** what I needed to pay for the trip to Peru.

The check sat on my altar for a few days, soaking in the sacredness of the moment before making its way to the bank.

I began researching flights, hotels, spiritual retreats, and the Cusco area. I didn't dive too deep. Just enough to get a sense of direction—enough to begin imagining an itinerary.

But strangely... a strong desire to book the trip was still absent.

Monday, July 1st, 2024.

This morning, I was scheduled to meet with Victoria—a colleague who has become a dear friend. As I stirred awake, I reached for my phone to send her a quick confirmation text for our 10 o'clock appointment.

To my surprise, I found a message already waiting for me: Victoria needed to reschedule. Rather than respond by text, I decided to call her. We exchanged warm greetings and a bit of small talk before I offered Wednesday, July 3rd, as a new date to meet.

That's when she told me she couldn't—because she was going to **Peru.**

Not just anywhere in Peru, but to **Machu Picchu.**

I was in awe. Another synchronicity. Another mirror.

As she shared her travel plans, I told her about mine—about the dream, the voices, the signs, the check. About the call that had become a certainty. She was fascinated. We agreed to meet up after both our journeys, excited to exchange stories from the Sacred Land.

Later that night, around midnight, I opened my laptop. It was time to begin.

The first thing I booked was the spiritual retreat. I had already narrowed it down to one, but my decision was more than research-based. Nearly two years ago, a dear friend recommended a place called **Etnikas**. Her words were glowing, and her experience unforgettable.

Etnikas is a spiritual retreat nestled in the Sacred Valley of Peru—specifically in San Salvador, Cusco. The memory of her testimony lingered in my heart, and it became the confirmation I needed. I booked it.

Next came the flights.

Etnikas requires a two-day stay in the town of Cusco before participating in any Ayahuasca ceremonies, to allow the body to acclimate to the altitude. It's a safety precaution—one I respected deeply.

I searched flight after flight from Fort Lauderdale. I had multiple options for departure, but none of them aligned well with the connecting flights into Cusco. The timing was always off. Nothing clicked.

And still, I refused to even consider flying out of Miami International. In my mind, Miami meant chaos—traffic, crowds, deep breaths just to get through it.

After two hours of searching through countless sites, I shut the laptop.

Not out of frustration—but out of trust.

The path was unfolding. I didn't need to force it.

Tuesday, July 2nd, 2024.

This morning, I was asked to visit an assisted living facility to help the Administrator complete some overdue medical forms. Apparently, the state had come in and noticed that several evaluations were outdated.

One of the primary care providers and I were sent to assist. The task was straightforward: if a recent medical evaluation had already been completed, we'd simply transfer it to the proper form. If not, we'd assess the resident and complete it from scratch.

Simple enough—except we were working with a population of nearly 100 residents, and the Administrator in question had once resisted having medical providers in the building at all. This was not just a logistical assignment. It was a soul appointment—one I recognized as an opportunity for transmutation.

Backstory.

I met this Administrator—let's call her *Sandra*—a couple of years ago, when I was still an Administrator myself, working for the same company. I had stepped in to help manage the facility just before she officially took over. My first impressions of her were that she was tough, a bit uncouth, and not exactly warm.

Over time, I began to understand more.

Two company holiday parties gave me deeper insight. At both, I observed her husband sitting silently in a corner, scowling. He didn't smile, didn't interact with anyone. At the second party, I walked over to shake his hand—and he practically barked at me:

"Can't you see I'm eating?"

For a split second, I felt anger rise. Then Malik's hand gently rested on my low back, centering me. I took a breath, offered a polite pardon, and walked away. I turned to Malik and said,

"If he behaves like that in public, imagine how he treats her in private."

From that moment on, I began extending Sandra more compassion. I remembered the times I had given my own power away in relationships. We are all mirrors of one another.

A few weeks after that holiday party, Sandra and I began texting here and there—checking in, small talk. Especially after she confided in me that her husband had left her for another woman. I sensed her deep relief laced with a subtle sting of rejection. She was free, but not untouched.

I didn't know then that those exchanges were laying the foundation for today—the day I'd walk into her building not as a rival, but as support. For someone as strong-willed and independent as Sandra, having corporate bring in an outside vendor like our team was likely a blow to her pride. But the goodwill we had already established made my presence feel more like balm than intrusion.

Truthfully, I was looking forward to being there.

And as the universe would have it, the day unfolded with surprise after surprise—each one kissed with synchronicity.

As I turned the corner into Sandra's office to greet her, I was stunned to see my friend Victoria standing there. Neither of us knew the other would be at this facility.

We embraced, both amazed by the serendipity. She began to share more details of her upcoming trip to Peru, including her plans to visit Machu Picchu.

She asked if I had booked my flights yet. I told her about my late-night search, and my internal resistance to flying out of Miami. That's when she reached for my hand, looked me straight in the eye, and said with full presence:

"Just fly out of Miami."

Victoria was the messenger—and I chose to receive the message.

That evening, in a span of just 20 minutes, I booked all four flights, as well as hotel and hostel stays. I was fully in flow.

And in the days that followed, the signs continued—angel numbers, repeating sequences, and constant references to Peru.

The path was clear.

I was going.

The sacred journey had already begun.

Wednesday, July 3, 2024.

I returned to the facility that morning to finish the assignment: updating the residents' medical forms.

As I exited the building, I noticed a Nissan Altima parked under the port cochere. The license plate read NEE E55. My breath caught. In numerology, the letters N and E each correspond to the number 5—meaning the plate could be interpreted as 555 555. The number 5 is often associated with change, freedom, exploration, and adventure.

I was so taken by the synchronicity that I snapped a photo of the plate and quickly texted it to Malik.

As I continued walking toward my car, parked about 50 feet away, I looked up and saw a bluejay perched in the tree directly above it.

Since my mother's transition in May of 2019, bluejays have always reminded me of her. I felt her presence immediately. I stopped, inhaled deeply, and allowed myself to receive the love pouring into me. My simple allowance became my offering of gratitude. Why resist a blessing?

It was a quiet, contemplative drive home.

That evening, I attended an Access Bars Exchange. For those unfamiliar, Access Bars is an energetic modality comprised of 32 points on the head that, when gently touched, release stored thoughts, emotions, and limiting beliefs. These points are connected to themes like control, creativity, money, sexuality, and more.

To be a Practitioner, you must take a full-day class. I trained with Yvette, an incredible Rolfer who introduced me to Access Bars.

An exchange is a gathering of Practitioners who meet to give and receive sessions. Tonight's was hosted by Yvette at her spacious, three-story townhome in Fort Lauderdale. Her entire first floor is dedicated to her healing practice.

Walking in felt like stepping into sacred space. Seven massage tables were neatly arranged side-by-side with enough room for fourteen attendees to move and work with ease. Each table was covered in a fitted sheet, adorned with a pillow and fuzzy blanket. The vibe was warm, intentional, and alive.

I took a moment to soak it in, then wandered into the kitchen and fixed myself a plate of rice and vegetables. I had already started my ayahuasca dieta—a plant-based, intentional diet in preparation for the ceremony at Etnikas. With the retreat just under three weeks away, I was gently adjusting my body to the new rhythm.

I chatted briefly with a few guests, but I mostly kept to my usual new-environment mode: observe, be still, and allow connection to come naturally.

When it was time to partner up, a young brunette stood near me. I smiled and tapped the massage table—a silent invitation. She accepted and lay down.

She received first. When it was my turn, she ran my Bars while Yvette sat at my feet and performed a Body Process[22].

The session lasted about an hour and fifteen minutes, but the trance-like state it induced made time feel irrelevant. I was floating in a place of stillness, clarity, and subtle recalibration.

When it ended, I slowly blinked open my eyes and took a few grounding breaths before stepping off the table.

Yvette greeted me. "How have you been? What have you been up to?"

I smiled, always game for a little shock-value humor:

"I listened to the voices in my head… and I'm going to Peru."

Yvette laughed. "I *love* it. The person who just ran your Bars—she's from Peru."

I turned to the young woman and introduced myself. Her name was Carolina, an acupuncturist originally from Cusco.

Goosebumps danced along my arms. Carolina noticed and smiled. Then she looked directly at me and said:

"They're waiting for you."

***

Since committing to Peru, my dreams have been active and layered. Two, in particular, stand out:

---

[22] An Access Consciousness Body Process is a hands-on method that uses different hand placements on various positions on the body while asking specific energies to run at each spot. These processes facilitate the body back into its original functions, which assist with the repairing and longevity of the body. The energies are the natural energies that bodies are and have access to from everywhere in the universe."
"Access Consciousness has discovered over 50 body processes: energies that can facilitate a body to change and transform. Each of these dynamic processes can be run as hands-on energy that invites the body to begin to heal and create itself." Information has been taken from
https://www.accessconsciousness.com/en/micrositesfolder/access-body/about-body/Body-Processes/

1. I was in an apartment labeled 304. Victoria, my youngest daughter (who is 16 in real life), appeared in the dream as a joyful 6 or 7-year-old, giddily sitting on my lap. Her older sister, Katelynn, watched and began to cry—throwing a tantrum. I called her over, hugged her, and invited her onto my other knee. Moments later, both girls began bouncing and laughing on my legs like they were riding a horse—pure, radiant joy.

2. The following night, I dreamt of Andrew (Victoria's father and my ex-husband). I was driving a Nissan Pathfinder—his actual car. A police officer pulled me over, suspecting the car had been stolen. Soon, Andrew arrived, followed by the actual car owner—my friend Nicole. Andrew gave me a look that said, *"What did you do now?"* But I didn't feel guilty. I remained silent. It all turned out to be a case of mistaken identity. Andrew didn't verbally apologize, but his face softened.

3. When I woke, I remembered something else: the tag on Andrew's vehicle also includes the number 555. Yet another divine thread leading me back to Peru.

***

In the days that followed, I stayed committed to the dieta.

Two weeks before an ayahuasca ceremony, participants are encouraged to follow a vegan diet, abstain from sexual activity (including self-pleasure), avoid recreational drugs, and steer clear of horror films or energetically disruptive media.

With the exception of a few hiccups, I stayed the course.

This was more than a physical cleansing. It was an energetic preparation for something sacred. Something inevitable. Something already in motion.

Friday, July 19th, 2024.
My flight to Peru was scheduled to leave Miami at 8:40 AM. Considering the drive from Dania Beach and the fact that it was an international flight, Malik and I decided to leave around 6:00 AM.

From the moment I arrived at the airport, the synchronicities began again. A quiet confirmation: this trip would be magical.

The flight left on time. With a layover in Panama City, I was expected to arrive in Lima by 4:00 PM.

It was my first time flying Copa Airlines, and my first international flight in years. Copa turned out to be a treat—warm, attentive staff, and yes, they offered meal service.

Breakfast was a bowl of creamy oatmeal, sweetened with brown sugar and topped with cinnamon, raisins, and coconut flakes. Small things like this matter to me. I smiled when they handed out free movies and headphones. I chose *Clash of the Titans* and immediately thought of my daughters—who, at eight and nine, were once obsessed with that movie.

We arrived early in Panama City. I had no checked bags, so I was able to walk straight to my connecting gate without waiting for luggage.

Every seat by the gate was taken, so I found a quiet corner on the floor nearby.

Even though the Wi-Fi at Tocumen International Airport was spotty, I managed to send messages to loved ones: "Halfway to Peru." I FaceTimed with Malik—knowing I might not have Wi-Fi again for a while.

Then, I just sat. Observing. Daydreaming about the retreat. Reminding myself: *This trip is sacred. This trip is magic.*

A Spanish-speaking voice over the loudspeaker eventually called us to board. Again, Copa's onboarding was seamless.

Once settled into my seat, I scrolled through the entertainment screen and chose a movie long enough to fill the flight. I picked *Constantine*. It felt like the right combination of mystery and distraction—something to keep my mind from whispering, *Are we there yet?* every five minutes.

Just as the movie ended, the descent into Lima began.

***

Though I'd checked the weather app beforehand, nothing prepared my body for the shock of the cold. Despite layering up with a camisole, long sleeves, and a thick poncho, the low 50s hit me hard. For a native Floridian who's seen snow only once, it was a moment.

Being fluent in Spanish helped immediately. I hailed a taxi and negotiated a fair rate with ease.

I checked into the Wyndham Hotel in downtown Lima. The accommodations were lovely—and to my joy, included a bathtub. I was already planning a hot soak in the morning before heading out into the cold.

I was only staying in Lima for one night. Tomorrow's flight to Cusco required me to be out the door by 5:00 AM.

It was 7:00 PM, and I was hungry. I did the math—four to five hours of sleep if I ate quickly, returned, and prepped for tomorrow.

I went downstairs to ask for restaurant suggestions. The most appealing option was a ten-minute walk near a mall with various restaurants. I chose the walk.

I closed my eyes, took a deep breath, and stepped outside. "This is mind over matter, Denise."

After half a block of self-hypnosis, the cold faded into the background, and like magic, I became fully present.

The streets were crisp and vibrant. I began to notice how I *towered* over most of the locals—despite only being 5'4". Later, I learned the average height in Peru is 5' for women and 5'4" for men. That explained a lot.

Next came the stares. With my Cuban curly afro and cowboy boots, I definitely stood out in a sea of jet-black straight hair. Some people stared. A few complimented my curls. I found it all amusing.

At the mall, I discovered an outdoor area lined with restaurants and, to my surprise, a third-floor food court that included Church's Chicken and TGI Fridays. I laughed and took photos to send home later.

But I hadn't come all this way to eat American fast food. Friends had raved about the Peruvian culinary experience—fresh ingredients, fusion cuisine, unforgettable flavors.

I chose a place with indoor and outdoor seating. Only outdoor was available. I braced myself for more cold.

To my delight, the patio was covered with overlapping umbrellas that trapped the warmth. It felt cozier than inside.

I chose a corner table with the perfect vantage point for solo dining and people-watching.

For dinner, I ordered a lacto-vegetarian salad: chopped romaine, plum tomatoes, large-kernelled Peruvian corn, a medley of baby greens, fresh house-made cheese cubes, and a center-folded avocado shaped like a flower.

The presentation was thoughtful. Beautiful. Sacred, even.

I began eating before the dressing arrived—couldn't help myself. When it did, a honey mustard vinaigrette, I drizzled it over the salad and took a bite with all the components. *Explosion of flavor.*

To drink: pure pineapple juice—no sugar, just blended fruit and water. The entire meal, with tip, cost seven dollars.

I walked back to the hotel, briskly this time to fight the colder night air. Traffic was light. People thinned out as I moved away from the mall. The final few blocks were quiet.

I passed one person. We exchanged polite nods and a "buenas noches." Then it was just me, my thoughts, and the cold streets of Lima, Peru.

***

I thought of the Pleiadeans.

Just before leaving for Peru, I'd participated in a rebirthing meditation with Johanne Rutledge, the medium who guided my early 2024 mediumship studies. After the meditation, Johanne received messages from healing entities.

They told her:

"She will learn about her roots. She will meet herself in another body."

I kept walking, repeating a favorite affirmation from Louise Hay:

"All is well. Everything is working out for my highest intention. Out of this situation only good will come. I am safe."

As I neared the hotel, I spotted José, the doorman who'd greeted me earlier. He wasn't Peruvian—maybe Dominican or Puerto Rican. As a fellow Caribbean soul, our connection was instant.

He smiled wide as I returned, the kind of smile my mother would say came from the eyes.

He asked how dinner went. I shared my joy and thanked him for the suggestion.

We made small talk, and he offered to help arrange a taxi for tomorrow. I politely declined, not sharing that Manuel—the taxi driver who brought me to the hotel—had already offered to pick me up at 5:00 AM.

Manuel had immigrated from Venezuela a decade ago with his wife. Their children were born in Peru. He was funny, warm, and kind. And now, he'd be my ride to the next stage of the journey.

***

Back in my room, I tidied up. Laid out my layers for the morning. Journaled. Read. Kept the energy soft and sacred.

When I felt sleep coming on, I turned off the lights, crawled under the covers, and smiled.

I had the heater on full blast.

Tomorrow, a hot bath awaited.

And then—the Sacred Valley.

Saturday, July 20, 2024.

I opened my eyes after only a few hours of sleep and felt amazing. I had woken up before my alarm with the same thought that had carried me to sleep: *my hot bath.*

Like a teenager buzzing with anticipation, I giggled aloud as I jumped out of bed and headed straight to the tub. I dipped a toe in, delighted to find the water perfectly hot—just enough to leave my skin rosy, sealing in warmth beneath the layers I planned to wear that day. I soaked for fifteen delicious minutes and felt wrapped in a blanket of heat all day, even once I arrived in Cusco, where the temperatures tend to drop more sharply than in Lima.

The hotel I had just checked out of was tucked in the quiet suburbs, but as soon as Manuel and I reached the city, I was surprised by how much traffic there was at 5:30 in the morning. Thanks to his skilled navigation, we made it to the airport in forty-five minutes.

The flight to Cusco was completely booked. The line at the booking counter was long, nearly forty people deep. I waited patiently, people-watching and soaking in the excitement. Many travelers were buzzing about their upcoming visits to Machu Picchu.

Despite the crowd, the universe orchestrated a seamless passage onboard. More attendants arrived, the line moved quickly, and I was soon at the counter. I learned I had only paid for a personal item and not a carry-on. With two backpacks in tow, I had to make a quick decision: $27 to bring it on board or $30 to check it in. I opted to pay the $27 to keep everything with me. It wasn't about the money, it was about the convenience.

By 7:18 AM, I was through security with nearly three hours until boarding. I chose a sit-down breakfast over fast food, wanting to remain grounded and nourished. The Spanish spoken here was slightly different from what I was used to, so I listened closely while ordering.

My meal was simple but soul-nourishing: eggs, potatoes, fresh fruit, and crusty bread baked onsite. The anise tea—bold, fresh, and aromatic—transported me to memories of my mother and Mireya[23]. My mother drank anise tea to soothe her stomach; Mireya, my dear friend, preferred it as a liqueur—Anís del Mono—served neat or over

---

[23] Mireya is a woman who took care of me while my mother worked. That would be from about 3 months of age until I was about 8-years old. She was our neighbor from across the street in Carol City, FL. She is a woman I love dearly. She is alive and approximately 88 years old. After the caregiving days during my childhood, I have remained in contact with her.

ice. She rarely drank, which made the memory feel all the more poignant and vivid.

At the gate, I noticed that there was no direct jet bridge to the plane. Instead, we boarded a bus that carried us across the tarmac to the aircraft. Once onboard, I was ready to dive into a book, but my body had other plans. The emotional energy of the journey had been catching up with me. I dozed off quickly and woke much later than planned.

When I woke up and finally opened my book, *Your Inner Shaman*, I noticed that I was surrounded by soccer players—members of Club Deportivo Garcilaso, a Peruvian team with plenty of players from Argentina.

The old version of me might have been dazzled by their athleticism and beauty, curious about their sexual energy. But the new me was watching from a different lens. I noticed their immature banter, jokes about lying to their wives to extend "practice" and euphemisms involving trampolines. Their bravado stirred something in me. A mix of anger and guilt rose to the surface. I had once followed sexual desire blindly. I had stepped out in all three of my past marriages. My past hypersexuality carried the weight of shame.

But I breathed through it.

I let the emotions pass and returned to *Your Inner Shaman*. As synchronicity would have it, I stumbled onto a section discussing the Divine Goddess who restrains her sexuality for fear of destruction. The reminder was gentle but clear: sexuality is a gift, not a curse. The time has come to transmute the negativity associated with my superpower.

Peru, I remembered, is said to hold the energy of the Sacral Chakra of the Earth. Emotions, creativity, sensuality, and flow—this land holds it all. I reminded myself: I am here to transmute, to shed old narratives, and embody a new story.

The book, whose complete title is *Awakening Your Inner Shaman: A Woman's Journey of Self Discovery through the Medicine Wheel* by Marcela Lobos, had entered my life serendipitously. Malik had encouraged me to buy it at Barnes and Noble. The synchronicities surrounding this book had already begun.

And now, just before landing, another one. I read a passage on page 107:

"I came to realize my legacy to my sons would not be memories of mom cooking three meals a day, seven days a week, and driving them around to birthday parties or sport games. My gift would be the example of how to follow the beat of one's heart, respecting and considering others, but not falling slaves to the incriminating voices of the past."

I began to cry. Openly. Unapologetically. That passage *was me.*

I thought of my daughters and how I raised them differently from how I was raised. Instead of sacrificing my dreams, I invited them into mine—swimming with dolphins, traveling, volunteering. I allowed them to explore beliefs rather than enforcing a single system. I have tried to teach them to follow their heart. Make them aware of their of their ability to create versus getting caught in the loop of the NPC[24].

My tears flowed. And just then, the Andes appeared, snow-capped and majestic. The pilot announced our descent. I looked at the time: 11:11[25].

We landed. I stepped into the crisp air of Cusco and hailed a taxi. Ten soles later, I arrived at my hostel—my first time staying in one. For years, I had avoided the idea, largely due to the horror movie *Hostel*. But now, after viewing images online, I had felt drawn to Kokopelli's Viajero Cusco.

The front entrance was simple: two large wooden doors with a brass knob that seemed pulled from another era. But the moment I walked inside, I gasped. The front atrium was breathtaking—warm wooden accents, Spanish tiles in rich burnt orange, and a peaceful, lived-in energy.

---

[24] Non-player character, a character in a game that is not controlled by a player. This term is often used a metaphor to describe someone who lack independent thought and blindly follows trends.

[25] "11:11 angel number stands out as a powerful symbol of spiritual awakening, new beginnings and divine guidance." Taken from www.otterspirit.com "Understanding Angel Number 1111" published July 18th, 2024

Three young women greeted me at reception. As I checked in, I found myself thinking of Malik. I imagined him enjoying this place—then an old voice rose inside: *Why would you bring him here, surrounded by all these women?* It was a familiar fear, rooted in past betrayals. I knew it wasn't about Malik. It was about me.

I recognized the guilt. The fear that I didn't deserve happiness because of my past. I returned to the message I had received in Johanne's rebirthing meditation: You do not need to pay a price to receive blessings.

Check-in was seamless. For just $14 a night, I was placed in a shared room with ten cozy pods built into the walls. Each pod had a curtain, crisp white linens, a shelf, and two outlets. Lockers labeled with painted letters corresponded to each pod. I purchased a lock from reception and stowed my things.

Ready to explore, I began with the hostel itself—over 200 years old. Soon I was joined by Paul, an engineer from the UK who had just come from the Swiss Alps. His partner is a psychiatrist, and as we spoke, our conversation took a deep turn.

We discussed *The Octopus Man*, a novel about a man living with schizophrenia. I shared my belief that people diagnosed with schizophrenia often experience a thinner veil between realities. What if they're not broken? What if they're simply receiving information from realms we cannot see?

We both agreed: these experiences deserve empathy, not dismissal.

After our enlightening exchange, I wandered toward the city center. The Plaza de Armas, Cusco's historic heart, welcomed me. I noticed a familiar voice arise—the part of me that seeks validation through male attention. But I reminded myself: *I am the Alchemist. I am creating this experience. Let me love myself through it.*

For dinner, I found a small restaurant and ordered the trout. It arrived pink and tender, paired with crispy potatoes and diced tomatoes and onions.

But back at the hostel, my body rebelled. I vomited violently—a full purge. The trout hadn't sat well. I FaceTimed Malik for comfort, but had to rush to the bathroom mid-call. When I returned, my head throbbed. I lay in my pod, nausea swirling, head pounding.

Another purge. This time, pure acid.

I listened to my body. I honored it. I thanked it for speaking so clearly.

I brushed my teeth and returned to bed. I focused on my breath. Deep inhales of divine love. Deep exhales of discomfort and dis-ease. I repeated this rhythm until sleep embraced me.

When I woke a few hours later, the headache had melted. I whispered my gratitude into the quiet.

I was being prepared.

I had crossed the threshold.

Sunday, July 21, 2024

I woke up feeling completely recovered from last night's ordeal with the fried trout. Determined to start the day on a positive note, I headed to the shower at the hostel—only to be met with a couple of unexpected challenges:

1. **Forgotten Towel:** In my haste, I'd forgotten to bring a towel.

2. **Uncomfortably Cold Water:** What began as lukewarm quickly turned ice-cold. July mornings in Cusco hover near freezing, with daytime highs only reaching the mid-sixties. With my Florida body and the lingering vulnerability from being sick, the cold stung especially hard.

Resourceful as ever, I used a camisole to dry off, slathered lotion onto my shivering skin, and dressed in layers to reclaim some warmth. Thankfully, the hostel's setup wasn't fully communal—just one shared stall. Still, I was grateful to get through it.

Once I was wrapped in enough warmth to feel human again, I dropped off my toiletries and made my way upstairs to the hostel's restaurant for breakfast. The meal was simple and perfect for my healing stomach: plain scrambled eggs, homemade bread, and a bowl of fresh fruit. Comforting. Nourishing.

Afterward, I lingered with a cup of anise and mint tea and read more from *The Inner Shaman*, letting the words sink in. Eventually, I felt a familiar pull to nap.

I curled up in my cozy little cubby bed, but just as I was about to drift off, I remembered a dream I had the night before—one that featured my mother. I reached for my journal to capture the details.

In the dream, my mother and I lived together. She looked younger—maybe in her early forties. I seemed to be in my late teens or early twenties at most. The math made no sense, since she gave birth to me just days before her 40th birthday, but dream logic doesn't bother with timelines.

We were out somewhere with her boyfriend, who appeared to be younger than her. She was performing fellatio and asked me to be on the lookout, since we were in public. In a blink, we were back at home. My older sister, Dulce, walked into the room and started asking my mother a string of pointed questions—almost like an interrogation.

Then Dulce turned to me and asked, "What about you?"

I looked at her, wide-eyed, and said, "What do you mean, *what about me*? I was the lookout."

That's all I remember. I closed the journal and finally allowed myself to rest.

I didn't recall dreaming during my nap. I woke just in time to use the restroom and make my way down to the front lobby for the street tour—led by Danilo, the man with the kind eyes.

Monday, July 22, 2024

I woke up too excited to sleep in—eager to begin this transformative journey. Once again, breakfast was simple yet nourishing: granola and fresh fruit. Gold star for me for continuing to eat exactly as the retreat center recommended.

I walked about ten minutes from the hostel to Plaza Nazarenas, where I met the twelve other retreat participants. Together, we boarded a spacious 16-seater Mercedes-Benz van. The ride wound its way up into the mountains toward the retreat center, nestled in the heart of the Sacred Valley.

When we arrived, the view took my breath away.

From our rooms, we could see the majestic snow-capped mountains stretching into the sky. The entire landscape radiated sanctity, as if Pachamama herself was calling us to slow down and absorb her ancient, living wisdom. I felt a wave of emotion sweep over me and, without resistance, I let myself cry. Tears of pure gratitude. I was in the presence of divine energy. I could feel it.

Today would be the first of three ceremonies.

Before our evening meditation, we each met privately with the retreat's psychologist, Marjorie. She had a warm, grounded, and approachable energy—setting a gentle, supportive tone for the days ahead. It was immediately clear that this would be a space for deep healing—mentally, emotionally, and spiritually.

Interestingly, I found myself talking about sexual trauma with Marjorie and started to cry. I told her I was ready to "see the dark side" of my childhood experience. I also shared that I'd been dreaming of my mother since arriving in Peru. I had no idea just how much was about to unfold.

The first dose of Ayahuasca was about a quarter of a shot glass. After drinking it, I felt a bit queasy—but that was it. I got up to use the bathroom. Still nothing. So I decided to take a second shot. Again, some nausea, but no purging. That didn't surprise me. The last few times I've sat with Ayahuasca, I haven't vomited—I've gotten the runs instead.

I could feel my stomach gurgling, but didn't need to go to the bathroom just yet. Then, the voices started.

Messages I received:

- *You harness the power to create worlds. Why choose to be a victim?*

- *You are a Divine Goddess who creates in love.*
- *You are sultry.*
- *You deserve to feel pleasure.*
- *Give yourself permission to be the woman you already know you are.*

Then came visions of myself embodying the victim archetype. Scene after scene, showing me moments when I played that role.

I looked at that version of me and said: "I love you. You've served your purpose. But now, you must leave. I choose to take my power back."

I don't know how much time had passed when I realized I had to go to the bathroom. Just as I stood, one of the staff members appeared—like magic—by my side. She must've sensed that I was groggy. I made my way to the bathroom and released. It felt incredibly cathartic. I chuckled to myself. Apparently, I'm becoming a "pooper" at these Ayahuasca ceremonies.

Side note: During the ceremony, I kept hearing a voice encourage me to smoke the sacred tobacco—100% pure Mapacho. But I felt resistance. I'm not sure what that means yet. If I feel the nudge again tonight, I'll follow through.

Back in the bathroom…

As I sat on the toilet, I began to observe the stall walls. Geometric patterns appeared and dissolved, shifting like sacred holograms. Then I saw a static-like fuzz in the air—reminiscent of an old-school TV turning off. It felt like reality was collapsing and rebooting again and again, as if I was doing this with my own thoughts.

It reminded me of that *Rick and Morty* episode where Rick builds a toilet sanctuary on another planet—his private throne where no one else is allowed. What starts as a ridiculous sci-fi gag turns into something deeply revealing. That toilet isn't just about control or comfort; it's about the illusion of isolation as a safeguard against vulnerability. I understood that. Because in that stall, I too was in a kind of multidimensional sanctuary—where the veil was thin and the sacred geometry of my mind was doing its own private ceremony.

Then I heard the voice say: *See? You are the creator.*

I cleaned myself up and made my way back to the mat. I buried myself in the warm den I'd created from blankets and continued receiving.

The voice repeated:

- *You are a Divine Goddess who creates in love.*
- *Give yourself permission. You are in control.*

For what felt like hours, I whispered over and over:

- *I give myself permission to be the Divine Goddess who creates in love.*
- *I give myself permission to trust in love—to be open to love and all things amazing.*

Eventually, I had to use the bathroom again. The visions were calming by then. When I returned, the ceremony was over.

Outside the maloca, a group of us stood waiting to be checked by the doctor. My vitals were good: blood pressure 110/60, pulse 67, and pulse ox 93%. The doctor explained that, at this altitude, anything above 85% is acceptable. I passed with flying colors.

I sipped some tea and listened to others share their stories.

John. I'm curious about him. My intuition tells me he may be transgender. As I stood there, I heard a message in my mind: *If you accept yourself, she will accept you.* I knew the *she* referred to his mother. I felt an intuitive nudge to share the message with John. When I did, he burst into tears and collapsed into my arms.

Tonight's experience reminded me of my mushroom journey on April 22, 2024—the day I had the epiphany about marijuana. The day I cleared my closet of entities. The day I cleared my closet of guilt.

Tuesday, July 23, 2024

Last night, I took two quarter-shots like before. Tonight I decided to dive in and take the half-shot of Ayahuasca from the get-go.

It took about an hour to kick in—though that's just a guess, since we weren't allowed phones or clocks in the maloca. The ceremony began in the dark, timeless container of the sacred.

For the first thirty to forty minutes, I spent time talking to myself to keep from overthinking. I gave myself Reiki, cycling through all twelve hand positions—four on my head, four on the front of my body, and four on my back. I paid special attention to my left hand and left thumb. I later remembered that, in energetic anatomy, the thumb represents intellect and worry. It felt fitting.

When the Shaman reached the front of my mat and began singing her Icaros directly to me, I felt her voice reverberate through my entire being. As she moved away, the Ayahuasca activated.

Suddenly, I could smell Malik. I imagined him in front of me, naked. I was naked, too. My hands, my mouth—they reached for him. The rhythm of the Icaros became the rhythm of our connection.

I caressed his thighs and took him into my mouth. I stroked him with my tongue, my fingers, tasting the sweetness of him. I was intoxicated by his scent, his presence, his essence. Slowly, I guided him to the ceremonial bed stretched before us and straddled him. As I let his deliciousness slide inside of me, I placed my hands on his chest and began to move.

Our eyes were locked. Our breath was in sync. The experience was primal—and profoundly spiritual. Orgasm after orgasm washed through me. He came with such intensity that he passed out the moment his body released its final drop. I collapsed onto him, wrapped in ecstasy, laughter, and love.

As the music faded, the vision of our bodies began to dissolve.

Then, the mind began to creep in:

- *What if he's cheating?*
- *What if he's playing with your emotions?*

But I silenced those voices with the messages I had received the night before:

- *I am a Goddess who creates in love.*
- *I give myself permission to receive unconditional love.*
- *I choose love.*

I pulled the blankets up over me, giggling like I did during my first mushroom trip. That same giddy feeling returned—the realization that *this is all in my head*, and that this is where the power lies. *The Mad Hatter is the Magician.*

These new thoughts held strong. I experienced no nausea, no purging.

I began to think of my mother. I remembered what I'd received through the Angel Board: that releasing guilt would open communication.

My initial intentions for this ceremony were:

- To communicate with my mother.
- To connect with extraterrestrials or higher-dimensional beings.

I began whispering to myself, gently anchoring into peace:

- *All is well. Everything is working out for my highest intention.*
- *Out of this situation, only good will come.*
- *All is well and I am safe.*

Then, thoughts of my medical job surfaced. Though I enjoy managing the practice, my soul wants something else. My soul wants to grow my spiritual work. While lying in the maloca, under the vine's guidance, I saw clear visions:

- Buy a massage table.
- Print a business card.
- Advertise.
- Meet with Helen to discuss a podcast.
- Plan retreats—Peru will absolutely be a destination.
- Create a Meetup for workshops:
    - Intro to Natal Astrology
    - Create Vision Boards
    - Intro to Spiritual Alchemy
- Create a free Reiki circle.
- Spend more time drawing and sketching.
- I kept repeating: *I write books.* Plural.
- I saw myself exercising in the mornings, continuing to embody wellness.

Then, I received the final vision of the night:
A *Chakana*. The Inca Cross.

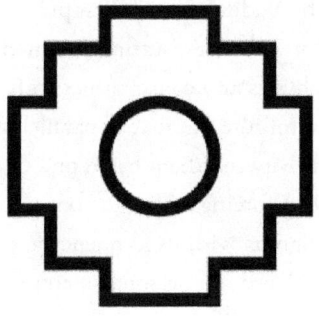

The image appeared so clearly in my mind's eye. I felt drawn to its geometry, its wisdom. I later reflected on how perfectly it aligns with everything I believe in: Reality Transurfing[26], spiritual alchemy, universal law.

The Chakana is derived from the Quechua words *chaka* (bridge) and *hanan* (tall), symbolizing a bridge between realms. It represents the interconnectedness of the cosmos.

Its stepped design points to the three realms of existence:

- Hanan Pacha (Upper World): The realm of the gods, higher consciousness, and divine guidance.

- Kay Pacha (Middle World): The human experience, the here and now.

- Ukhu Pacha (Lower World): The subconscious, the ancestral realm, the underworld of transformation.

- Each realm is associated with an animal:

- Condor (Hanan Pacha): Divine vision, expanded awareness.

- Puma (Kay Pacha): Strength, courage, presence.

---

[26] The phrase "Reality Transurfing" originate from the Russian metaphysical book series **Transurfing Reality** by Vadim Zeland, first published in 2004. Zeland, a former quantum physicist, presents Transurfing as a model of reality based on quantum mechanics, metaphysics and consciousness principles. At its core, Reality Transurfing suggests that an infinite number of parallel realities exist simultaneously, and we shift between them based on our thoughts, emotions, and energy alignment. Rather than forcing reality to conform to our desires, we "surf" into the desired reality by aligning with its frequency and reducing "pendulums" – external energetic structures that drain personal energy. The phrase itself implies fluid movement through different life tracks rather than rigidly controlling reality – akin to surfing the waves of existence rather than struggling against them.

- Serpent (Ukhu Pacha): Transformation, renewal, the shedding of skin.

- These worlds mirror the Hermetic principle: *As above, so below. As within, so without.*

- The Chakana also aligns with the four elements and cardinal directions:

- Earth (North): Grounding, stability, manifestation.

- Water (West): Flow, emotion, intuition.

- Air (East): Wisdom, intellect, the breath of life.

- Fire (South): Transformation, will, creative power.

At its center lies a circular hole—the portal of unity. The zero point. The place of conscious awareness where all duality dissolves and infinite realities converge.

The Chakana, I realized, is a tool for spiritual transmutation. It teaches us that by aligning with divine principles, we can shift timelines, move between realms, and live from a place of conscious creation.

It is a mirror of my own becoming.

When we heal ourselves, we harmonize with the entire cosmos.

Wednesday, July 24, 2024
Integration day – no ceremony scheduled

I woke up with the sniffles. Not sure where they came from.

Actually, now that I think about it, they started last night—little sneezing fits that came in waves.

By morning, my nose was stuffy and I could feel a head cold forming.

Given how I was feeling, I decided not to join the others in volunteering at the animal shelter. I let myself sleep in.

When I finally rose and walked around, I noticed many participants had stayed behind too.

One in particular was Song—a South Korean quantum physicist

living in New York. He was sitting outside the maloca, writing. His current project: a book about the Merkabah, its energetic points, and his interpretation of their metaphysical meaning.

He was excited to share. As of today, he had written fourteen pages.

He was writing on his MacBook. I picked it up and began reading—his ideas were profound, original, and beautifully expansive. As I read, I thought about *my* books—plural. I *know* they've already been written in another realm.

At that very moment, I looked down and saw "**222%**" in the lower right corner of his screen.

I immediately teared up.

Two memories came flooding in—two sacred confirmations of my authorship across timelines:

1. **Logan from Crystal Vision** – She told me I was surrounded by Pleiadians, and that in several other realities, I was already a published author.

2. **Thoth meditation** – The voice within said: *You've read all the books. You've written all the books. You are one with all.*

That moment with Song, in the sunlight of the Sacred Valley, was yet another breadcrumb—another sacred nudge reminding me who I am.

Afterward, I took a break to rest. With no ceremony scheduled, it was the perfect time to integrate.

I sat in an Adirondack chair just outside my room and looked out over the valley.

The air was cold, with a soft breeze. But I was bundled in layers, topped by the Peruvian poncho I've worn during every ceremony.

This poncho has a story.

I bought it in the fall of 2023, anticipating a local Ayahuasca ceremony. I found it at a thrift store in Hollywood, Florida—but it was *new*, with the tag still on. The moment I saw it, I felt it had been waiting for me.

Since that day, it has carried sacred energy. I've had three profound moments where white feathers were not just near it—but actually *intertwined* in the fabric, as if woven there by Spirit.

- The **first feather** appeared during that initial Ayahuasca ceremony. A quiet sign of divine presence—a message from Spirit that I was held and guided.

- The **second** showed up during a Reiki circle. Again, it gently rested in the threads. I felt it as a clear affirmation that my healing work was divinely supported.

- The **third** came during a mediumship course. This one felt like a direct bridge between realms. It wasn't just a sign—I felt it in my bones: *I am the medium.*

What always struck me is that the feathers weren't simply lying on the poncho—they were woven into it. To me, that's more than a message. It's an embodiment of how deeply Spirit is integrated into my path.

These weren't random signs. They were acknowledgments:
You're walking in alignment with something higher. Something sacred.
And now, here I was, in Peru—wrapped in that same poncho—gazing at the majesty of the Andes.

This same fabric, infused with story and Spirit, was keeping me warm as I sat in awe of the Sacred Valley.

I eventually drifted off into a nap, held by mountains and memory.

When I woke up, I joined the others for dinner, grateful for the nourishing meal the staff had prepared.

A new group had arrived at the retreat, and a handful of the original participants had left.

While we dined in the common room, the new group began their first Ayahuasca ceremony.

Later that evening, those of us from the original group gathered by the firepit.

The Shaman had spent a good part of the afternoon chopping firewood for us. The fire was blazing strong.

Aside from the small ground lights that lined the walkways, the fire was the only source of light.

And the sky—oh, the sky.

You could almost see the Milky Way stretching across it. *(Photos of this night sky are included in the appendix.)*

Among us was Bic, from Canada. As we were talking, I noticed his phone case.

It had his contact info printed on the back.

His street address?

222.

Another sign. Another whisper. Another *yes*.

Thursday, July 25th, 2024
Final Ceremony Night

This morning proved to be eventful.

Bic wasn't feeling well. He'd been coughing and experiencing shortness of breath. The final straw was when his oxygen concentration dropped to 60%. He was taken to a hospital in the city shortly after.

In the afternoon, we received massages.

After reading the last page of Song's draft, I took some time to myself to set my intentions for the final ceremony of this retreat:

- Connect with my mom
- Connect with extraterrestrials
- Receive inspiration for my first book
- Connect with Solomon
- And… release the sniffles completely

I kept telling myself: *I feel healed.*

But my mind needed a pause. I took a slow walk back to the room before the evening meditation.

During the walk, I repeated:

- *I am a Divine Goddess who creates in love.*
- *I give myself permission to create an amazing life.*
- *I deserve love and abundance.*

I thought of my daughters, Katelynn and Victoria. How much I love them. How amazing they are.

I wondered—What does Victoria want to do after high school? What is her passion?

And then I smiled, thinking of Katelynn's strength—the way she always finds her way, even through the storm. She carries a wisdom far beyond her years.

Then I thought of Malik. How much I love him. How deeply I am in love with him.

I crawled into bed for a short nap—just enough rest to prepare me for what was to come.

And I'm glad I did.

Because what came next was one of the most profound journeys of my life.

The DMT moved through my veins like never before. The effects lasted around nine hours.

I took a ¾ shot around 7:30 p.m.

I connected with:

- My mom
- Nidia
- Millie

- Stephanie's mom
- Daniel
- Ayana's grandmother

Messages I received:
My Mom:

- *My name is Denise*—she named me after a French author she admired.
- I'm meant to write a book simplifying *spiritual alchemy*.
- I had not written the book before because I didn't feel that I was an authority on spiritual alchemy. She then tells me "who more so that you is an authority of your own joy?"
- *She loves Malik.*

Millie:

- *Erick, please forgive yourself.*

Stephanie's Mom:

- I've never met her. I don't know her name. I don't know what she looked like.
- *She loves Stephanie deeply and is incredibly proud of her.*
- *She sees what an amazing mother Stephanie is.*

Daniel:

- *Malik has been patiently waiting for the return of his playmate.*
- He thanked Malik for loving me.

Ayana's Grandmother:

- Like Stephanie's mom, I never met her. I've seen photos, but I didn't recall her name or face.
- Yet, she came through. Softly. Clearly.

***

By 1 a.m., I had left the maloca and returned to my room, still very much in the medicine. I sat upright near the top of the bed, placed one hand on my belly and one on my heart, and began to breathe—slow, deep, diaphragmatic breaths. With that breath alone, the visions restarted.

They carried me until 5 a.m.

The whole night felt like a multidimensional reunion—a convergence of souls, messages, timelines, and truths.

It was a final ceremony, yes. But also a beginning.

Friday, July 26th, 2024
Travel Day to Aguas Calientes

This morning we took the van to the train station, though the journey didn't go quite as planned—many of the streets were closed due to a local parade.

The van had to park several blocks away, so we walked the rest of the way on foot. There was something grounding and real about it—being among the locals, weaving through celebration and movement on our way to something sacred.

The four of us boarded the train from Cusco to Aguas Calientes.

I absolutely loved the town of Aguas Calientes.

The charm. The energy.

The bridge covered in locks.

The stream flowing right through the middle of the city—like a heartbeat.

By the time we arrived, we walked around, had lunch, shopped a bit, and then headed to dinner.

Our hotel was simple and cozy. I noticed a fire extinguisher hanging on the wall with a printed number: **762222**.

I didn't go looking for angel numbers. I rarely do.

But then, like always, I heard that unmistakable voice in my mind: *"Look."*

And when I looked—there it was. 222. Again.

The universe keeps whispering. And I keep listening.

Saturday, July 27th, 2024
Machu Picchu Day

We took the bus from Aguas Calientes up to Machu Picchu.

The ride itself felt sacred—like ascending into another layer of reality.

Both Song and I could feel the energy shift as soon as we arrived.

It was palpable. Ancient. Thin-veiled.

I began seeing visions.

Incas walking among us.

An Incan woman kneeling beside a stone, grinding grain with deliberate reverence.

Above one of the structures, I saw a spaceship hovering—silent, watchful.

It felt like the dimensions were overlapping. The veil between worlds had dissolved.

Another wink from the universe.

After checking into the hotel, we went out to eat.

The front desk staff had recommended a restaurant called **"Cocina Sin Secretos"**—translated: *Kitchen Without Secrets*.

The phone number? **084 222219**.

And when we arrived, the server introduced himself as **Salomón**—Solomon, in Spanish.

Another layer of confirmation.

Another divine nod.

The Sacred keeps revealing itself—always hiding in plain sight.

Sunday, July 28th, 2024
Final Day in Cusco – Peru's Independence Day

I woke up that morning thankful for the warm night.

I had a private hotel room with central heat—an unexpected comfort after so many nights in chilly hostels.

The four of us gathered for the complimentary breakfast at the hotel, savoring one last meal together. Afterward, we parted ways.

I walked back to the same hostel where my journey in Cusco had begun.

A full-circle return.

After checking in, I made my way to *Malqui Tattoo*, a studio in Cusco known for its clean lines and sacred ink.

I got a tattoo of the **DMT molecule** on the inside of my left forearm.

A permanent reminder of everything I had experienced.

Everything I had remembered.

Afterward, I returned to the hostel for a quick nap.

When I woke up, I walked to Plaza de Armas to meet up with some of the guys from the retreat.

We had dinner at a restaurant with a second-floor balcony that overlooked the plaza—a gorgeous, historic wooden terrace glowing in the evening light.

After dinner, Song invited us to *Palacio Nazarenas*, a luxury hotel just across from Plaza Nazarenas. He had booked two nights at $1,000 per night and wanted to treat us to dessert in the courtyard.

I ordered a rich chocolate cake served with warm coconut milk.

It was divine.

I knew the next day would be long—three flights ahead of me:

From Cusco to Lima, Lima to Panama City, and finally from Panama to Miami.

So I decided to walk back to the hostel.

The streets were lively and congested. Artisans had set up kiosks along the sidewalks, selling handmade crafts and colorful knick-knacks. I didn't stop to ask anyone for directions—I just walked, letting my intuition guide the ten or so blocks back.

When I arrived, I discovered there were more festivities planned for the evening.

As it turned out, **July 28th** was **Peru's Independence Day**—*Fiestas Patrias*.

The entire country celebrates this day, honoring General José de San Martín's declaration of Peru's independence from Spain. The energy spills across every city and pueblo, with parades, flag ceremonies, traditional music, and folkloric dances.

At the hostel, a celebration was in full swing.

Inside the restaurant, a stage had been set up where young Peruvians danced in vibrant, colorful attire.

I stayed for about an hour, simply observing—taking it all in.

The music, the movement, the joy.

Eventually, I returned to my room.

I packed my things and laid out my clothes for the morning.

Grateful.

Full.

Ready.

Monday, July 29th, 2024

Return to Miami

Early that morning, around 6 a.m., I left for the airport.

Saying goodbye to a magical city.

To the mountains that whispered.

To the spirits that spoke.

To the land that remembered me.

But the magic didn't stay behind.

It followed me home.

My final flight arrived in Miami at **22:29** local time.

Another wink.

Another 222.

Another beginning.

Post-Journey Reflection
(*August – December 2024*)

In the months that followed my return from Peru, I began planting seeds.

I started writing this book.

I recorded three podcast episodes.

I printed business cards for the Reiki center.

I enrolled in art classes—and dance classes, too.

The turning point came during an Afro-Cuban dance class on Saturday, August 10, 2024.

There were only four of us in the room.

That day's dance was dedicated to the Orisha **Babalu-Ayé**—known in Christianity as **San Lázaro**. A beloved and powerful deity, revered for his healing abilities.

His dance, like his myth, is rooted in restoration, in the resilience of the body and spirit.

Something shifted in me during that class.

As we moved, something unlocked.

I began to cry—a deep, guttural cry that came from a place I didn't even know needed release.

I couldn't fully process the freedom I was feeling.

Afraid of the unknown that was now expanding within me, I found myself reaching for something familiar.

That same evening, after months without marijuana, I picked some up.

That moment marked the beginning of a stretch of smoking sessions that would continue until December.

It was as if the surge of healing cracked open a doorway... and I wasn't quite ready to walk through it sober.

That return to an old habit prompted me to revise sections of this book—especially the chapter titled *The Voice, Alan Watts, and the Roaches*, where I reflect on my complex relationship with marijuana.

During this time, I also reconnected with Debbie (*name changed*), who would later become my travel companion for my second trip to Peru in January 2025.

We started talking about Peru in August, during one of our smoke sessions.

She wanted to go for her birthday in January.

Shortly after setting the intention, she booked her flight. I noted the flight number—but didn't make my own travel arrangements. Not yet.

Debbie kept reminding me to book. But her reminders didn't feel loving.

They felt like echoes from a former version of myself—one that was constantly being corrected or scolded.

Instead of getting defensive, I silently thanked her—for highlighting a part of me that still carried emotional charge. She became a mirror. An opportunity to respond differently.

She joked that she would finish her passport application and I wouldn't—meaning I wouldn't be able to go with her.

I smiled and said: *It'll all happen in divine timing*.

Because it would.

I still needed to book my flights.

I still needed to reserve my spot in the retreat.

I still needed to renew my passport.

But I had already received the nudge:

The wave was forming.

I just had to jump—and let the universe deliver everything I needed.

Thursday, December 12th, 2024
The Call to Prepare

After a morning meditation, I received a clear message:

It was time to **pace myself** and begin initiating my travel arrangements.

Another message followed closely behind—an inner nudge to begin the **detox**.

I took out a sheet of notebook paper and began listing the things I wanted to accomplish in the coming weeks:

- Book four flights:
    - Miami → Lima
    - Lima → Cusco
    - Cusco → Lima
    - Lima → Miami
- Book the retreat. Once again, I'd be returning to **Etnikas**.
- Renew my passport.

That very day, I called the Miami passport office and scheduled an appointment for Tuesday, December 31st at 7:00 a.m.

Yes, that meant I would be placing full trust in divine timing—relying on that single appointment to receive the passport I would need for my flight scheduled just **three days later**, on **Friday, January 3rd, 2025**.

And yet, I felt calm.

Aligned.

Certain that everything would unfold as it should.

Sunday, December 15th, 2024

I booked the Etnikas retreat and the connecting flight – Lima to Cusco and Cusco to Lima.

Monday, December 30th, 2024

Choosing the Flight, Trusting the Timing
Today I searched for a flight to Lima.

Debbie had already booked hers through Avianca, with a connection in Bogotá. But based on what I'd heard, Avianca didn't compare to Copa—the airline I flew in July. From personal experience and the feedback of friends, Copa stood out for a few reasons:

- Friendlier, more attentive staff
- Cleaner, more comfortable planes
- Better in-flight entertainment (every seat had a screen with free movies)

So rather than follow my intuition—and my preference—I booked with Avianca.

After securing the flight, I reached out to Debbie and let her know I was officially set.

I also reminded her that I'd be going to the passport office in the morning for my December 31st appointment. I couldn't help but smile at the irony:

She had once joked about me failing to renew my passport in time… and now here she was, telling me she *still hadn't received hers*.

She asked if I'd go with her so she could follow up in person.

I agreed.

The whole thing made me laugh a little inside—how timing, trust, and the universe always seem to flip the script just enough to reveal what's really going on beneath the surface.

Tuesday, December 31st, 2024
Passport Office & a Pocketful of Grace

I picked up Debbie around **5:30 a.m.** so we could beat the traffic into downtown Miami. Thankfully, we arrived just in time for my **7:00 a.m.** passport appointment.

At check-in, Debbie was turned away by the security guards—she didn't have an appointment.

She waited outside while I went in, using the time to call the passport agency and check the status of her own passport.

After a brief wait, I was called to **Window 22**, where I was met with unexpected enthusiasm by the clerk.

I handed her my flight itinerary and the receipt for my retreat at Etnikas.

The transaction went smoothly—almost effortlessly. I was instructed to return at **10:30 a.m.** to pick up my passport.

When I stepped outside around **7:30**, Debbie had just gotten off the phone. She told me her passport had been processed—it had officially been *purchased* and was **out for delivery**.

We had some time to kill, so we decided to grab breakfast at *Bistro Café*, a spot just down the street.

The café was about a 15-minute walk. Just before we arrived, my phone rang.

A woman with a thick accent was on the other end.

She told me she had found my **wallet, ID, and keychain** near the passport office.

Apparently, it had fallen out of my pocket without me realizing it.

We turned around and headed back.

Debbie was in disbelief—not just that I hadn't noticed it was missing, but that someone had found it and decided to return it.

The woman had looked inside the wallet, found my *Reiki business card*, and decided to call the number. She waited for us by the sidewalk, holding my things with a kind smile.

Grateful doesn't even begin to describe it.

We thanked her and headed back to *Bistro Café*.

Let's just say… our breakfast **did not** follow the Ayahuasca dieta.

I'll be the first to admit—I had **two mimosas**.

There was humor and grace exchanged between us. No judgment. Just presence.

By **10:30**, we were back at the passport office. Full bellies, good spirits, and a light heart.

Minutes later, I walked out with a crisp, freshly printed **passport in hand**.

When we returned home, Debbie was still waiting for hers.
It finally arrived later that evening.
Because of course it did.
Right on time.

Wednesday, January 1st, 2025
New Year, Familiar Faces
My friend **Alisson** came to visit today.

There's a long history between us—many stories woven over the years.

In fact, it was through Alisson that I met Debbie.

This time, Alisson stayed with Debbie.

And truthfully, I was genuinely excited to see her.

The last time she came to visit was in December 2021, during a particularly difficult chapter of my life. She stayed with me back then.

Emotionally, I was in a fragile place. And I remember feeling like she ripped into me during that visit.

Looking back, I can see how I may have attracted that kind of energy—I wasn't extending myself much grace at the time.

Still, I believe she could have chosen kindness. She could have met me with more compassion.

But that was then.

A few years have passed.

And I've been through *many* transformations since.

Which is why I felt different about seeing her now—more grounded, more emotionally spacious, more myself.

I was in a better place.

And because of that, I could meet her without fear or armor.

Thursday, January 2nd, 2025
A Familiar Face at Publix
I ran into Saul today at Publix.

I can share a bit of his story here.

We first met around 2017, back when I was still working in the insurance industry.

We were both attending a grant writing class hosted by the Hollywood Chamber of Commerce.

Not long after that, I left the insurance world and transitioned into a role in the sales department of an assisted living facility.

Even with the shift, Saul and I stayed in touch.

In 2021, he reached out to me with a temporary opportunity.

He needed someone to oversee Midtown, a residential program, while he took his wife to Hawaii for her birthday. The plan was for me to help out for two weeks.

But two weeks turned into much more.

I ended up staying on at Midtown, eventually moving from Site Supervisor to Executive Director.

As I shared earlier in the book, I stepped down from that position in January of 2024.

So running into Saul today—on the eve of a new journey, just before flying back to Peru—felt like another full-circle moment. A quiet reflection of how far I've come.

Friday, January 3rd, 2025
Return to Peru – Round Two Begins

Malik took Debbie and me to **Miami International Airport** to catch our flight to Bogotá.

Let's just say my research proved to be spot on: **Avianca Airlines** was a sharp contrast to Copa.

Here's a quick recap of the experience:

- The staff felt *snooty*, cold, and unwelcoming
- No meals included on the flight
- All food and drinks had to be purchased—even water

- Yes, they would give you a small cup of water *if you asked for it*. But after that? You had to pay for more.

Definitely not Copa.

***

Over the next couple of days, Debbie and I spent time settling into **Cusco** and our **Airbnb**, which sat high on the mountainside.

The view of the city at night was breathtaking—twinkling lights stretched across the valley like constellations below our feet.

I didn't journal much the first two days. It was cold.

Really cold.

I don't even remember if we ate dinner that first night. Maybe we were too tired. Maybe it was just too late by the time we got there.

On Saturday, January 4, we had breakfast and did some shopping. Later that day, we went on an ATV tour to two popular tourist destinations: the salt mines and a sacred site called Moray.

At Moray, we met our guide Carlo—a soft-spoken man with powerful energy.

As soon as we entered the site, I felt it: goosebumps.

Something about that place... it felt like a vortex. A thin place between dimensions.

On Sunday, January 5, we celebrated Debbie's birthday by getting tattoos.

We returned to Malqui Tattoo, the same shop I visited during my first trip.

Debbie got three tattoos.

I got a small llama on the back of my left tricep, just above the *Follow the White Rabbit* tattoo I already had.

Another layer. Another symbol. Another thread in the woven story of Peru.

Monday, January 6, 2025.
The Return to Ceremony – Balance, Honey, and the Quantum Heart
The morning began with a vegetarian meal in the center of the Plaza.

After breakfast, we made our way to **Plaza Nazarenas**, where the van picked us up for the retreat.

There were sixteen participants in this group.

I found it interesting how many of them were smokers—something that stood out right away.

That evening, we participated in our first ceremony.

We began around 6:00 p.m. with a meditation. I loved the recording they played—Albert Einstein's letter to his daughter, where he speaks of love as the strongest frequency in the universe.

By 7:00 p.m., the shamans were preparing to open the ceremony. That's when I noticed a white feather in my blanket.

A familiar sign.

I asked for ¾ of a shot of Ayahuasca.

Soon after drinking, I began to feel the physical effects—but no messages were coming through.

One of the nurses came over and gently said, *"Just relax… it'll come."*

Moments later, I heard a voice:

"What are you resisting? Learn to flow like honey. You are pure, sweet, and delicious."

My hands instinctively began to caress my body. I started thinking of Malik, of making love to him.

The energy was sensual, electric.

I felt powerful, fully in tune with my sacral energy.

I let myself get lost in the feeling.

What felt like an hour of lovemaking passed through me, until I heard the voice again:

"Balance."

A series of visions followed—each exploring the theme of balance between the physical and the spiritual. Then came another message:

"I am you. Ayahuasca is a tool."

Suddenly, I began thinking about a girl named Honey.

I must've been around 11 or 12 when I made fun of her name—and my father was furious with me.

In this moment, I saw myself visiting Honey.

Interestingly enough, I had looked her up before this trip. According to Google, she's a financial planner in Miami Lakes.

I started thinking about her father.

I couldn't tell if he had transitioned, was alive and estranged, or alive and simply wanted to share something.

Then I heard:

"I named you Honey because I knew you were pure sweetness and love."

I felt it—a surge of pure love between a father and a daughter.

I began to cry.

Visions continued—this time around themes of insulation and protection. I felt myself praying. I felt myself shaping energy, like I was becoming my own sacred container.

I am more than my body.

I am beautiful, sexual, sensual—and I will not dim my light for anyone.

I remembered how, after my first trip to Peru, I had been working out and losing weight.

One day, a stranger looked at me in a way that made me feel like a piece of meat. It shook me.

I stopped showing up for my body after that. I dimmed.

But tonight, I reclaimed something.

Midway through the ceremony, I had a massive purge—so strong that it came out through my nose.

The shamans and nurses quickly came to my side.

One of the shamans performed a protection ritual.

He used a bundle of sacred plants, tapping and brushing them gently across my body. Then he used two different types of floral water, taking each into his mouth and gently spitting the mist across my body as he brushed me with the plants.

Once the ritual was complete and the shaman moved on, I sat up—and heard another voice:

"You are a builder. It is important for you to understand the SPECTRUM of emotions—not to wallow in them."

A wave of messages followed, all around compassion:

- *All is happening now.*
- *Resistance creates a lag in reality-building.*
- *We are transmuting all "past lives" and their infinite versions—plus all infinite versions of this life, and every doppelgänger.*
- *A shift in reality can happen in the blink of an eye.*
- *Time is the human experience.*

Tuesday, January 7, 2025
Victor, the Burn, and the Thunder Within

We were all gathered in the conversation room, sharing our experiences from the previous night.

Before the facilitators formally opened the circle, some of the participants were engaged in small talk. I was in my own world, journaling, when I overheard Jordan, one of the guests from Florida, mention something about shooting a coyote.

"*They're pests,*" he said casually.

A wave of anger surged through me—sudden and unexplained. It rattled me.

Then there was Ilya.

He had the air of Rasputin—long, disheveled hair, and a presence that felt both magnetic and untamed. His hygiene was questionable, and yet... something about him drew my attention.

When Ilya began sharing a story about an unborn child—a child his girlfriend had aborted—I became unexpectedly emotional.

I've never had an abortion in this life. And yet, I found myself crying.

Then I thought of Victor.

Victor is a male child I terminated in a *previous* lifetime. Here's the story:

When Malik and I first started dating, Victoria (my daughter) would occasionally see the spirit of a little boy wandering outside our bedroom door. A few weeks after his first appearance, Malik and I consulted the Angel Board to ask about him.

According to the board, his name was Victor.

In that lifetime, Malik and I were living in Germany. We were having an affair. I became pregnant. Malik didn't want to continue the relationship, and in my hurt and anger, I chose to end the pregnancy.

When I first became aware of this past-life memory, I was flooded with emotion—grief, regret, sadness, all of it.

Sitting in that conversation room in Peru, something clicked.

A knowing.

That Victor and Victoria are energetically connected. That perhaps… the soul returned, or at least remained near.

That evening's ceremony began with a meditation.

Another white feather appeared in my blanket. I took the same dose as before—¾ of a shot of Ayahuasca.

A few minutes after drinking, the hot water bottles were distributed. Mine was placed on my right hip.

But the bottle hadn't been sealed properly.

Within seconds, scalding hot water began to leak out. It soaked through my clothing and burned the skin on the inside of my right hip—just near the groin.

I screamed.

The team rushed over to help. The skin was visibly irritated, inflamed.

The burn covered an area about 4 square centimeters.

I sat in stunned silence for a few minutes, trying to bear it—but eventually asked to get up.

Samantha escorted me to the bathroom. I stripped away my layers—including my *Stitch onesie*. When we looked at the skin, it was red and angry.

I started crying.

"Why is this happening to me?" I asked, through tears.

Samantha wrapped her arms around me.

"Remember," she said gently, *"everything happens for a reason."*

That's when I thought of *Louise Hay's Heal Your Body*—a resource I've used and shared countless times, including with this group.

Here I was, sharing wisdom with others… and now the lesson was for me.

Physician, heal thyself.

According to Louise Hay, burns represent anger.

And yes, I had felt it—raw, sharp, and electric.

At Jordan.

At life.

At the unnamed shadows within me.

Outside, a thunder and lightning storm was rolling in—ominous and poetic.

When Claudia brought me another hot water bottle, I declined—loudly, firmly.

As I did, a bolt of lightning flashed through the windows, lighting up the room.

A literal illumination.

The theme of the ceremony became clear:

Choose love.

Even if that means loving my own rage.

Even if that means honoring what once burned me—inside and out.

Because anger served a purpose.

It protected.

It revealed.

It asked to be seen, not shamed.

Tonight, I didn't reject it.

I welcomed it home.

Thursday, January 9th, 2025.
The Cat, the Claws, and the Victory

I woke up very early—must've been around 5:30 AM.

Changed clothes. Crawled back into bed.

I placed my hands on my body and began to perform Reiki on myself.

Then I opened the book Simeon had given me: *Veronika Decides to Die* by *Paulo Coelho.

I didn't know Coelho had once been in a mental asylum. That truth lingered as I read—quietly rebellious and raw.

Dare to be different.

Later, I went downstairs and sat with the retreat cat, Puma.

She climbed onto my lap and stayed for about 30 minutes.

When she finally stood to leave, she dug her claws into my left knee.

It wasn't an attack—it was a message.

The word that echoed in my ears was: flexibility.

As the day unfolded, I noticed myself feeling irritated over a few small incidents.

Nothing dramatic—just enough to stir discomfort.

What does flexibility mean to me?

Where do I resist flow?

How is that tied to trust?

Then came the internal reminder:

Ask with clarity.

Be in the frequency to receive.

That's when I felt Millie.

Her presence was near—warm and grounding.

And I connected with my Higher Self.

I heard a voice—steady, knowing, loving:

Denise, you know there are other realms and other dimensions. But get your head out of the clouds. You chose to be human.

Let yourself have the human experience.

***

And then came the night.

And with it—Ayahuasca.

And DMT.

The DMT flowed through my bloodstream like a river of light.

I felt it awaken me from the inside out.

While many around me were purging, I found myself laughing out loud. Giggling, smiling. Not from disrespect—but from the sheer ecstasy of remembrance.

Even after the ceremony officially ended, I could still feel the medicine working through me.

Back in the room, I continued to ride the wave.

One of my roommates made a comment about my breathwork—perhaps a bit confused by how I was still so activated.

I smiled and said simply,

"I came across the world for this DMT. I'm going to enjoy it."

And I did.

The visions kept coming, wave after wave of insight.

But one stood above all the rest—

My guide came to me and spoke, clearly and with love:

"La Victoria es tuya."

"Victory is yours."

And I knew.

I had done it.

I had crossed the threshold.

All that was ever required of me was to have fun

and trust the unfolding.

A Reflection

After the final ceremony, I stopped journaling about the trip.

Debbie and I experienced some tense moments toward the end. In her, I saw reflections of patterns I was actively working to release. It was uncomfortable, yet illuminating. I realized that these parts of me don't need to be exiled—they need to be met with love and grace.

Since returning from Peru, our relationship has been quietly evolving into something different. Rather than forcing clarity or defining what it needs to be, I'm allowing it to take shape on its own, in divine timing.

One thing did become clear: I stopped smoking marijuana. In that newfound clarity, I noticed our common ground had shifted. Not out of judgment—just resonance.

I've chosen to focus on my unfolding, my healing, and my joy, while still holding space for Debbie in my heart. There is love here—unconditional, quiet, and full of patience. Not every relationship has to be loud to be sacred. Some just need room to breathe.

Chapter Ten

MESSAGES FROM HER

I thought I had written the last chapter in the Sacred Valley of the Andes. I thought the story had reached its crescendo among the mountainous skies, among ancient spirits and whispered prayers. But the truth began to unfold before the ceremony even began, on the evening of April 4th, 2025.

It started with a woman – The shaman's mother, stern and inquisitive. When she questioned me, I felt myself shrink – not in fear, but in something deeper. I became small again. Soft. A little girl wanting to be seen and understood, not scolded.

And instead of retreating into hurt, I leaned into her presence.

I asked myself, *What does she represent? Why is this moment stirring something in me?*

She opened the door.

I had always been the doorway.

But it was through her question that I stepped into the space where my inner child waited.

And because I didn't flinch, the veil lifted.

And that night, I met her – the one who had waited for me all along.

April 4th, the night the ceremony began, marked the first time I had volunteered – or more accurately, been asked to volunteer – at the ayahuasca sessions. The shaman, sensing my readiness, felt it was time for me to step into a new role, to work alongside the participants.

The process included an element of detox, not unlike the preparation required for the ayahuasca participants.

I adhered to the guidelines, with only a few exceptions: I had some alcohol that week, and I'd had sex a couple of days before the ceremony. Aside from that, I felt grounded in my choices – a diet free of animal products and processed foods and free from marijuana, which I had not smoked in months. When I arrived at the spiritual center, I changed into comfortable clothing, not knowing exactly what I was supposed to do as a volunteer. While I had read the volunteer manual, the specifics of my duties weren't included.

I arrived first, ahead of the three other volunteers, and was greeted by the shaman's mother with what felt like a cold reception. She made small talk, though I could sense a deeper layer of expectation beneath her words. After I changed into my "work" clothes, she told me to start working through the duties. I explained that I didn't know what was expected of me because the volunteer handbook didn't provided a detailed list of task.

The look she gave me left me feeling small, as if I had done something wrong, as if I was unprepared and taking the responsibility too lightly. She didn't say it directly, but I felt it in her gaze.

The other volunteers arrived soon after, and they greeted me warmly. They assured me we would work together to complete the tasks at hand and showed me where the list of duties was kept. The list of duties was laminated so that we could tick off the completed tasks using a laminated marker.

For the next few hours, we kept busy: refilling kerosene lamps, chopping fresh fruits, restocking napkins, and one of my personal favorites – creating a flower mandala in the Maloca, the sacred space where the ceremony would be held. It was a meditative process, and for a moment, I allowed myself to lose track of time, absorbed in the rhythm of it all.

But then came the moment that changed everything.

As I was getting ready to change into something light-colored for the ceremony, the shaman's mother looked me up and down. "You brought a change of clothes, right?" she asked, her voice almost disapproving. Before I could respond, she continued, "If you had read the manual, you would know that white is required for all ceremonies – not just for the participants but for the volunteers as well. If you need something white to wear, there are outfits to choose from in the closet of the room where you will be sleeping."

Her tone struck me. it felt more like a reprimand than guidance. It was so different from the ceremonies I had attended in Peru, where the focus was always love and the inner journey, not the outward appearance. In Peru, participants were encouraged to dress comfortably; the staff wore dark blue uniforms, and the shamans were beautifully adorned in their native attire. There was not emphasis on the color of clothes, only on the intention to connect with the divine to remind us that we are pure love.

In contrast, here, the constant conversation centered around healing, sorrow, and releasing something holding us back from becoming our highest selves.

I found myself asking her, genuinely curious, "What's the logic behind everyone wearing white?" She spoke, but didn't really answer my question. I probed further, wanting to understand. The more I asked, the more her answers seemed to lack clarity, and the frustration in her voice became palpable.

Then she said something with a tone that hit me like a stone. "Girl, don't you know that when people are depressed, they typically wear dark clothes? They see the darkness. The white represents the light we are working towards."

I heard her, yet didn't understand. We are the light.

I felt a rush of emotions surge within me – hurt, confusion, and a subtle anger. Her words weren't as much of an issue as her tone, which felt condescending and dismissive. The inner child in me recoiled, wanting nothing more than to curl up in a corner, away from her scrutiny.

Instead of reacting, I chose to observe. I took a deep breath and retreated to my room. Instead of putting on the clothes I had brought – light-colored, including a white shirt – I chose to wear what had been set aside for volunteers in the closet.

When I came back out, she looked at me and, almost absentmindedly, referred to me as a "girl" again. This time, I couldn't let it slide. "My name is Denise," I said, firm yet calm. "And if you are addressing me directly, I would prefer you use my name rather than calling me 'girl'."

As I turned to walk away, she called me back into the kitchen and began asking me questions that I wasn't expecting – questions about my past.

"Have you been watching pornography?" she asked bluntly.

I was stunned. Not only had I not watched pornography in years, but why in the world would she ask me such a thing? Then she went on to interrogate me about the last time I drank, used marijuana, or watched the news. She said that she didn't want me to "ruin the ceremony" because, according to her, there is a significant exchange of energy in these rituals, and she didn't want anything negative from me to interfere.

The mix of emotions inside me was overwhelming: hurt, confusion, and a strong desire to defend myself. But then I paused. I reminded myself that I had created this moment. She wasn't attacking me – she was merely a reflection of something within me that needed love.

I understood then: The inner child in me was craving love. She wasn't just a shaman's mother; she was a mirror. Her behavior, though uncomfortable, was a reflection of the unresolved emotions within me – the parts of myself I still needed to nurture.

As I made my way to the Maloca, the warmth of the evening air wrapped around me, and I couldn't help but feel a deep sense of gratitude for the natural beauty surrounding the center. Nestled in 15 acres of land, the property was simple, yet abundant in life. The mature trees stood tall and wise, their gnarled branches reaching toward the sky, reminding me of the Ents from the *Lord of the Rings*. They were like ancient guardians of the sacred space, silently watching over the land, and I could sense they held the power to guide us to unseen portals, connecting the physical world with spiritual realms. A small man-made pond glistened in the fading light, reflecting the magic of the moment. Despite the unpretentiousness of the place, I found solace in its simplicity, and with each step, my appreciation for the environment grew. The gentle hum of nature filled the air, and in this stillness, I began to feel grounded, connected to something greater than myself.

When the ceremonial bell rang, signaling the gathering, we volunteers filed in and stood alongside the shaman, who stood before the circle of participants. A stillness settled over the group as we began with the brief introductions. The shaman then spoke of the purpose of ayahuasca – of healing, insight and the journey. His voice carried a deep sense of calm.

He also went over some important housekeeping rules for the ceremony, such as the necessity for silence once the journey began, the importance of staying close to one's mat, and that the participants should call upon the volunteers only if absolutely necessary. He reminded us to maintain the integrity of the space and to be present for the participants throughout the evening.

As the sun dipped below the horizon, one by one, the participants took their shots of ayahuasca. Each person then made their way to their mat, where they would spend their evening alone with their journey, guided only by their inner experiences. After all the participants had settled, it was the volunteers' turn. The ritual was simple: though the dosage was less than what the participants received, the volunteers too would partake, enough to allow us to stay connected to the ceremony and assist as needed.

I took my shot, the bittersweet liquid sliding down my throat, its taste lingering in the back of my mouth. As I settled back into my chair, I closed my eyes, trusting the process, and prepared to embark on my own journey. About thirty minutes later, the effects began to stir within me – a subtle shift in perception, the edges of the world softening and bending like the breath of a gentle wind. It was only the beginning, and I instinctively knew that the ride ahead would be long and profound.

At this point, some of the participants had already begun experiencing the effects of the plant medicine. A few had already started purging, releasing emotions or physical blockages in their bodies – a powerful reflection of their desire to rid themselves of what no longer served them. watching them, I couldn't help but reflect on my own journey with the medicine. Over time, I have learned to embrace every part of myself, even the aspects I had once rejected. This deeper self-acceptance had transformed my perception, leading me to a profound appreciation for the collective consciousness that binds us all together, the shared energy that moves through and connects us.

Suddenly, a need to move arose, and I decided to get up and use the bathroom. As I exited the Maloca, the world around me seemed to ripple in and out of focus, and I knew this was only the beginning of the night's unfolding. Something deep within me stirred, and I could feel the energy of the ceremony wrapping around me, ready to take me somewhere I could not yet understand.

I returned to the Maloca after using the restroom, a sense of euphoria washing over me. My experience with the medicine has taught me to surrender and allow it to work its magic, rather than forcing any particular outcome or attempting to purge parts of myself. Tonight, I knew it would be no different.

I found my seat and bundled myself up in my Peruvian poncho, feeling the warmth and comfort of its fabric as the ceremony continued around me. As I settled in, the medicine began to work, and a flood of images came rushing forward.

One after another, I saw my youngest daughter, Victoria, her face vivid in my mind's eye. I could hear her yelling and screaming at me, a mirror of the unhealed places in both of us, especially during those tender years—ages nine through twelve—when my voice, instead of soothing, often echoed my own woundedness.

The guilt came rushing back, heavy and suffocating. I had long since forgiven myself for those moments, but the remnants of that shame and guilt still lingered, festering just beneath the surface. In that moment, I felt all of it – every ounce of remorse and regret. This guilt was not only present in the images of my daughter but also in the realm of reality around me. As the other volunteers moved about, assisting the participants, I found myself frozen in my chair. Under the influence of the medicine, I couldn't bring myself to get up and assist. The DMT coursing through me made it impossible to act, and I felt this helplessness, this inability to contribute as I had expected.

Rather than allowing these emotions to drag me down a path I no longer wished to walk, I realized something profound: this was all part of the illusion that the medicine was showing me. It was not meant to keep me trapped in guilt but to redirect me, to guide me toward healing my inner child.

What struck me was that Victoria's anger was also a reflection of the anger I carried inside of me – the same anger that had been triggered in my interaction with the shaman's mother. In both cases, I felt the heaviness of unresolved emotions, and in both cases, it was clear that my own inner healing was the key to releasing this cycle. The reflection of this healing process was brought into focus by the exchange with the shaman's mother, mirroring the very emotions I was facing with myself. it was as if the universe was presenting me with a mirror, asking me to look at myself with love, compassion, and understanding. The journey of healing my inner child was unfolding before me, revealing the layers of hurt, the unresolved pain, and most importantly, the path toward forgiveness and self-love.

About two weeks before this ceremony, Malik and I had a sacred session using what many call a Ouija board – but ours is different. It's an *Angel* board, adorned with two ethereal beings, a portal for love and guidance. That evening, one of my guides gently suggested something I had not expected: "It is time for inner child work."

Interestingly, Malik had already been on that path. For the past few months, I have watched him courageously navigate the emotional landscapes of his own inner child. He didn't just talk about healing – he embodied it…leading by example. The way he faced his pain, sat with it, and moved through it with such tenderness and honesty – it moved me. My love and admiration for him grew in ways I didn't think were possible. He became a mirror, not only showing me what healing looked like, but giving me permission to dive deeper into my own.

Since that Angel board session, I had embraced this invitation from Spirit. I was drawn to guided inner child meditations and began a deep dive into the teachings of Louise Hay, especially *You Can Heal Your Life*. Her words helped me access places within my self that were ready to be seen, loved, and transformed.

As a daily devotion, I changed my phone wallpaper to a picture of myself at around five years old – little Denise. Each time I reach for my phone, there she is. Her bright eyes, her innocence, her whole world still ahead of her. I say to her out loud, *"I love you. You are safe."* Sometimes I kiss the screen, and it feels like I am kissing my soul. I remind her that I see her, and that I will always be here.

It's important I share this because during the ayahuasca ceremony – when the memory of Victoria's anger rose up like a storm, and the familiar guilt began to swirl around me – I could have chosen the path of fear. But this time, I didn't.

This time, I called in love.

I closed my eyes and summoned the image of little Denise. I walked toward her in my mind's eye, arms wide open. I embraced her. I told her: *"I love you. I see you. I want you to thrive, to love, to laugh, to play, to feel safe in this world."*

I stayed with her. I whispered truths, offered her comfort and let her be. I chose her – again and again. For what felt like hours, I held her close.

And then – it happened.

She spoke back.

She looked up at me with the most endearing eyes – so full of trust, so full of hope – and then she said something that caught me completely off guard.

"Hablame en espanol." Speak to me in Spanish

At first, I was surprised. Why Spanish? And then, like a flood of memory washing over me, I remembered: for the first few years of my life, Spanish was my heart's first language. Although I was born and raised in the United States, the rhythms and melodies of my early life were sung in Spanish. It was how I communicated love, fear, joy, confusion – it was the language of my earliest truths.

When I began school, I was placed in ESOL[27] classes during kindergarten and first grade. English came later. But in those formative years, it was Spanish that comforted me, that cradled me. And now, here she was – little Denise – asking to be spoken to in the language that once made her feel safe, seen and whole.

So I did.

"*Té amo, mi amorcito…Denisita, estas segura. Estoy aquí para ti siempre.*"

I love you, my little love…little Denise, you are safe. I am here for you, always."

As I spoke, to her in Spanish, I felt it wasn't just the sweet exchange between my adult self and my inner child. It was something far more profound.

It was a soul retrieval and a shift in my reality.

In the sacred science of spiritual alchemy, we speak of transmutation – not just of metals, but of the self. Lead into gold. Suffering into wisdom. Wounding into radiance. And in that moment, I could *feel* the alchemical process unfolding inside of me. As if the medicine had activated an internal crucible – where my subconscious emotions, my childhood grief, my long-held guilt, and my ancestral language fused into something higher, something lighter.

The DMT moving through my body became the philosopher's fire, burning away illusion and calcification. The image of my younger self – the child who once navigated life in a world that didn't fully understand her – wasn't just a vision. She was a catalyst. She was the prima materia, the raw substance of transformation.

As I hugged her in my mind's eye, as I whispered loving words in

---

[27] English for Speakers of Other Languages.

the language that once defined my earliest years, I felt the walls between time and space dissolve. I wasn't just remembering, I was *reconstructing*.

In alchemy, this is known as coagulation – the final step in which something new is solidified after purification. I was as if I had just gathered all the scattered parts of myself and anchored them into a new, more crystalline reality. The past had no hold on me. Not in the same way.

This was not just healing. This was spiritual chemistry in motion. A quantum recalibration of identity.

And it was all made possible by love.

After that energetic shift, a well of emotion rose to the surface – an ocean pressing up against the dam I had unconsciously built over years of guilt, shame, and self-protection. I felt the tears coming. My face quivered. My breath shallowed. I was about to weep.

But before the tears could fall, *she* – my inner child, little Denise – reached up with her small, warm hands and began to gently wipe them away. Her eyes, full of sweetness and strength, met mine with a clarity that took my breath away.

She whispered, "*No quiero que llores más. Quiero que juegues conmigo.*" I don't want you to cry anymore. I want you to play with me.

Then, with a lightness that felt like magic, she took me by the hand and led me inside a house – one I didn't recognize in this realm but that felt deeply familiar in the soul. It wasn't the house I grew up in, nor any I had ever visited. It existed in the liminal space between memory and imagination. It was *hers*. It was *ours*.

Room by room, she guided me through her sacred world. Each room was its own universe. She showed me sketches she had drawn – delicate, beautiful lines that spoke volumes. Paintings of animals, wild and free, adorned the walls. Picture books lined the shelves, books that she had written herself – her voice, her stories, her truths.

There was no pain here. Only wonder.

I felt as if I had stepped into a temple of her imagination – a museum of all the things she had been waiting to share with me. and she wasn't seeking my approval. She was *inviting my presence*. My playfulness. My love.

This wasn't just inner child work. This was an *invitation into joy*.

And the medicine held the space with the gentleness of a divine mother, allowing the full integration of the lesson to land in my heart. This was the great alchemical union – not just the healing of wounds, but the resurrection of creativity, spontaneity, and wonder.

This was the gold of my spirit, unearthed through love.

As the ceremony continued, I remained seated in the chair just outside the Maloca, bundled up in my poncho. The visions slowed down, but the emotional reverberations continued to ripple through my being. I had just experienced something so sacred, so intimate, that I felt a part of me had permanently shifted. The presence of my inner child, the love I felt for her, and the promise I made to continue nurturing her lingered like a gentle embrace.

I found myself in a state of elation – evidenced by an unstoppable wave of giggles that bubbled up from within me. It was as if the medicine had unlocked a portal of joy and lightness, and my heart couldn't help but overflow in laughter. I couldn't stop giggling, even as I felt deeply connected to my experience. My giggles were not just a release; they were an embodiment of the joy and freedom I had just touched within myself.

Around me, the ceremony was still unfolding. Some participants were deep in their process, purging or softly weeping, while others lay in stillness. The other volunteers moved in and out of the maloca, tending to the needs of the participants. While I was unable to assist physically, after this experience, I didn't feel any guilt. If anything, I felt that this was exactly what I needed in that moment – to focus on myself and my healing process.

The reality of the situation is, I feel as if, from a synchronistic standpoint, the true purpose of me volunteering was to have that interaction with the shaman's mother. That exchange triggered the lingering guilt and anger, and in turn, facilitated the deep healing I needed. Truth be told, I love attending the ceremonies as a participant

– it's where I feel most connected. And following such an impactful connection, I simply felt a strong journey to return home.

Malik, who has been instrumental in my journey, has a painting being displayed by the local Art Guild. It's not his artwork, but that of my dear friend LuRu[28]. LuRu has been a witness to this chemical process I have willingly jumped into, and she did a painting of me that embodies the fermentation process I went through. It's a beautiful piece, and it was actually displayed several months ago at the same venue, winning an award.

After the ceremony, I found myself focused on something more immediate – acknowledging the purpose that had been served and returning home to process everything. My heart's desire was to come back and write about the experience, to honor the shifts I had undergone, and to celebrate Malik's transformation as well. His painting is something truly special. It depicts him in a Kung Fu pose, morphing into an eagle – a beautiful representation of the journey he's been on and the strength he's cultivated.

As I spoke with one of the volunteers – interestingly enough, the same one who had been my roommate – she gave me some pushback when I expressed my intention to leave early. Although she lovingly insisted on having me stay, I held firm. I now truly understood that the purpose of my volunteering was to trigger this profound healing, not necessarily to be physically involved in assisting others at the ceremony. It was the journey inward, and now it was time for me to honor that space within myself.

As I reflect on this journey, I realize that the most powerful shifts often come from moments of discomfort. Daring to do something different despite the apprehension.

By stepping into the unknown, allowing myself to be observer of my own patterns, I unlocked a new level of healing. The discomfort was a catalyst, but it was how I responded to it that made all the difference. In choosing to embrace the uncomfortable, to witness the emotions that

---

[28]www.lurustudios.com

arose, I created the space for profound change. The beauty of this work lies in recognizing that when we pause – when we choose to respond differently rather than react – we unlock the potential for transformation. It's not always about the path we set out to walk, but how we walk it, and how we meet ourselves in those moments that define our growth.

Sometimes, the deepest healing happens when we allow ourselves the grace to step back, to observe, and to trust that by shifting our perception, we shift our reality.

The key to all of this for me came down to inner child work. Our inner child holds prima materia, the raw material from which all of our life experiences are created. The wounds we carry from childhood shape the narratives we tell ourselves and how we respond to the world around us. When we approach life with the enthusiasm of a child – unencumbered by the limitations of old stories – that's when the true magic of being human unfolds. Once we heal those early wounds and embrace the playful, curious nature of our inner child, life becomes a much richer, more vibrant experience.

It is through this work that we find the deliciousness of living, and in that shift, we find freedom – freedom to heal, to grow, and to truly live.

Afterword

THROUGH THE SMOKE: ALICE, OSHUN, AND THE ALCHEMY OF BECOMING

It was at a funeral in May of 2025 where the veil grew thinnest.

Not just the veil between the living and the dead—but the one between symbol and meaning, seen and known, form and spirit.

I hadn't expected to find magic there.

But magic found me anyway. It always does.

I had arrived to honor a life that had transitioned, surrounded by the sobering scent of flowers, incense, and cigarette smoke. The air was thick—not just with grief, but with presence. Spirit was palpable.

I saw the deceased, still tethered to the space—not in body, but in energy. Watching. Witnessing.

The family were Santeros—devotees of the Yoruba tradition. The room pulsed with Cuba's ancestral rhythms. In every glance, every prayer, every puff of smoke, the Orishas were present.

Almost everyone there smoked cigarettes.

But it didn't feel like a habit.

It felt like a hymn.

A sacred offering.

That's when I saw her.

A woman nearby, arm exposed—tattooed with a caterpillar resting on a mushroom, exhaling smoke.

In that smoke were the words:

"Who are you?"

It stopped me.

Not just for its surreal imagery.

But because it mirrored something I've lived.

Something I carry—not on my skin, but in my becoming.

I, too, have been asked that riddle, repeatedly.

Who are you?

Like Alice, I've followed the White Rabbit—uncertain where it would lead.

Only to discover it led deeper into myself.

Minutes after I left the funeral, as I am driving I remembered:

On my own left tricep, I wear a tattoo of Alice chasing the White Rabbit.

"Follow the White Rabbit," it says.

And down the centerline of my body—from cleavage to navel—I carry another sacred imprint: the symbol of Oshun, Orisha of rivers, gold, and sweet divine femininity.

She flows through me.

She *is* me.

As this realization landed, I turned a corner in my car after the funeral—and there they were:

Sunflowers.

A full stand of them, radiant and bright, right as I made a right-hand turn.

Sunflowers. Sacred to Oshun.

A directional blessing.

A golden **yes** from the Universe.

And right then—right after I saw the sunflowers—I remembered something else:

Earlier that week, my friend Mike had sent me an article about a groundbreaking experiment at CERN, the European Organization for

Nuclear Research. One of their detectors, serendipitously named ALICE, had documented the transmutation of lead into gold.

The very *heart* of alchemy.

It wasn't just science.

It was synchronicity.

It was the universe winking through physics, reminding me that the sacred is never separate from the seen.

Because that's what I had been living—alchemizing grief into grace, shadow into light, lead into gold.

And in that moment, I understood:

I *am* the experiment.

I *am* Alice.

I *am* the Philosopher's Stone.

I *am* the gold Oshun pours into the river.

I *am* the smoke rising, whispering "Who are you?" to the next brave soul who dares to look.

Featured Contributor Section

In this sacred journey of becoming, I've been blessed to walk alongside fellow seekers—kindred souls whose insights echo the deeper truths of the heart. Among them is Mike McKenney, a cherished member of my soul family whose wisdom has illuminated parts of this path.

His contribution to this work is offered below, and I invite you to receive it as part of the collective, remembering we are all here to do.

***

I'd like to thank my good friend Denise for providing this space. We met at an on-line Reiki circle, and I discovered she was into Bashar. We instantly clicked.

When I retired from working, I was excited to have time to pursue my two passions, Artwork and Spirituality. Little did I know that the two would combine in unexpected ways.

After I experienced Reiki for the first time, I became a Reiki Master in Gendai Reiki Ho. Because of this, my artwork evolved into subject matters like Sacred Geometry and Mandalas. The growth of my art serves as a physical benchmark of my spiritual journey. I receive inspirational ideas from within, not just for artwork but for spiritual wisdom as well.

I do not remember how it started, but in 2024, I discovered Bashar on YouTube. I liked his explanations of things, so I tried the permission slip exercises and meditations he offers. I was shocked to find that they actually made a huge difference in my life. By doing these simple things, I felt transformed like a butterfly emerging from its cocoon. I still don't understand how this was possible. How does Bashar possess such transformative wisdom?

I have never been a woo-woo person, so I just didn't focus on his ET claims. But I gradually came to realize that someone with profound spiritual wisdom has no motive to lie about other things. I now understand that the two areas are closely intertwined.

All of this brought me incredible Joy and my natural urge was to want to share this with people. But I discovered that many were not ready to receive it. So I created the basharfocus blog not only to share but to help crystallize in my mind the things Bashar was saying.

Here are some of the more interesting inspirations I have received.

***

Denise Perez

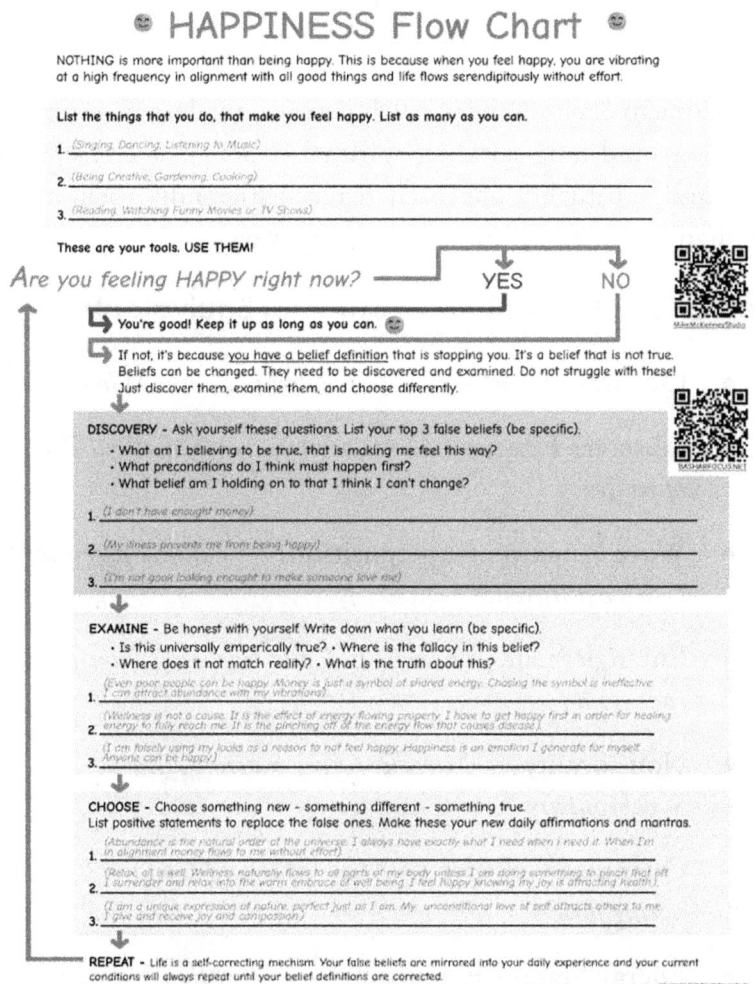

I was inspired by the teaching of Abraham-Hicks and Bashar to create a Happiness Flow Chart. It's a guide to help you pinpoint what beliefs are keeping you from experiencing Joy and replacing them with more truthful beliefs.

***

Below is part of an interesting chat I had with AI.

Quantum Physics and Spirituality: A Comparison of Concepts

This document explores the parallels between modern quantum physics terminology and long-standing spiritual or religious concepts. While science and spirituality approach reality differently, their metaphors often align in surprising and illuminating ways.

Bulleted List of Quantum ↔ Spiritual Equivalents

- **Quantum Field** ↔ *Divine Matrix / Source / God*
- **Observer Effect** ↔ *Consciousness creates reality / Power of prayer*
- **Wave Function (superposition)** ↔ *Infinite potential / God's omniscience*
- **Entanglement** ↔ *Oneness / Collective soul / Non-local connection*
- **Non-locality** ↔ *Miracles / Prayer across distance / Synchronicity*
- **Quantum Collapse** ↔ *Manifestation / God's will taking form*
- **Energy States / Frequencies** ↔ *Vibration / Chakras / Spiritual resonance*
- **Quantum Tunneling** ↔ *Instant transformation / Divine intervention*
- **Uncertainty Principle** ↔ *Mystery of faith / The unknowable divine plan*
- **Quantum Foam / Virtual Particles** ↔ *The void / Akashic field / Cosmic womb*

- **Multiverse / Many Worlds** ↔ *Heaven and Hell / Parallel lives / Karmic timelines*

- **Quantum Coherence** ↔ *Spiritual alignment / Unity consciousness*

- **Observer Consciousness** ↔ *Atman / Christ consciousness / Soul awareness*

- **Dark Matter / Dark Energy** ↔ *Holy Spirit / Prana / Unseen spiritual forces*

Comparison Chart

Quantum Physics Term	Spiritual/Religious Equivalent	Explanation
Quantum Field / Zero-Point Field	Source / Divine Matrix / God	Underlying field of all existence; formless potential
Observer Effect	Consciousness shapes reality / Prayer	Reality shifts when it is witnessed or believed
Superposition (wave function)	Infinite possibility / God's omniscience	All outcomes exist until one is chosen /observed
Entanglement	Oneness / Collective Consciousness	All things remain connected beyond space and time
Non-locality	Miracles / Remote Healing / Synchronicity	Influence across space without direct contact

Collapse of Wave Function	Manifestation / Divine Intention From potential into physical form	From potential into physical form
Frequency / Energy States	Vibration / Chakras / Auras	Our state affects what we experience or attract
Quantum Tunneling	Instant healing / Breakthroughs	Leaping through barriers via divine or energetic flow
Uncertainty Principle	Mystery of Faith / Surrender	Some things are inherently unknowable
Virtual Particles / Foam	Akasha / Spiritual void / Creative matrix	Invisible background seeding physical reality
Many Worlds Interpretation	Parallel lives / Heaven / Karmic dimensions	Multiple realities or timelines exist simultaneously
Quantum Coherence	Harmony / Inner alignment	Unified state of energy or being
Quantum Observer	Divine Witness / Atman	Awareness that shapes reality
Dark Matter / Dark Energy	Holy Spirit / Life Force / Prana	Powerful unseen forces shaping the visible world

Final Note

This comparison is not meant to equate science and religion directly, but rather to **highlight resonances** that allow for dialogue and deeper understanding. Both systems, when viewed humbly, point to a **mysterious, interconnected, and consciousness-responsive universe**.

For spiritual seekers, these parallels can validate intuition. For scientific minds, they may encourage respect for ancient wisdom traditions. For everyone, they offer a common ground to explore the mystery of existence.

***

Blueprint

The most important thing I have learned from Bashar is to identify and deal with the cause of my experience. The blueprint is the source plan from which everything else flows. Our blueprints are our belief definitions. Seemingly by magic, they are mirrored into our daily experience. Our beliefs that are in alignment with the truth of our nature, provide smooth experiences of synchronicity where good things automatically flow. But our beliefs that are wrong about our true nature give us experiences that are unpleasant. Most of these beliefs we have picked up from childhood, from our parents or others.

These unpleasant experiences are a message to us, telling us that something is off and needs to be addressed. Ever notice that you keep running into the same situations over and over? These energy patterns will persist until examined and replaced.

In the middle of an unpleasant situation, ask yourself:

- "What would I have to believe is true about myself in this situation, that is causing me to feel, think, behave, or experience what I am experiencing?"

Or

- "If I did in fact allow myself to be who I really prefer to be, what am I afraid might happen?"

With honest self-examination you will discover that your false beliefs seem silly or illogical. Once identified and examined, they can easily be replaced by more aligned beliefs. Positive affirmations and mantras help with this.

Your belief definitions are the blueprint, and you are free to change them to anything you want.

Your emotions are the builders of your reality.

Your thoughts are the building materials.

Your behaviors are the style in which the builders are building your experience.

Your experience is you living in the experience that was built from the blueprint.

This is THE KEY to understanding our reality, yet most people don't have a clue that life works this way.

***

Crown of Creation

I believe devout religious people have it wrong. Their belief that we need to worship God is backwards (like God needs his ego stroked). The truth of our existence is that All-That-Is (God) worships us, his children. We are nothing less than fully empowered agents of Creation. We expand the Universe (The Field) into infinite unseen energetic timelines and dimensional waves with our thoughts. This is not woo-woo, this is quantum science. The dimensions we experience are a collapsed wave, determined by our focus, belief and frequency. The Field rearranges itself around our frequency.

We are:

* Beloved

* Supported

* Empowered

* Adored

* Worshiped

We are aspects of All-That-Is. We are the crown of creation.

***

Self-driving Taxi

Let me give another analogy. You get into a self-driving taxi to take you where you want to go. You don't need to:

- Find your car keys
- Drive
- Put gas into the car
- Perform mechanical maintenance
- Give step-by-step directions where to turn

All you need to do is provide a clear explicit definition of your destination. Everything else is done for you. It's not your job. Just relax, chill and you'll find yourself at your destination.

And so it is with life.

***

The Greatest Event

We are in the midst of an ongoing, massive, revolutionary shift in our understanding of consciousness, even though it's not covered by news outlets. It's simply the greatest event in all of human history that is unfolding before our eyes. We are blessed to be witnessing and participating in the dawn of the New Age. Bashar says 2027 is the year *everything* changes. Future generations will look back on these times and marvel.

***

Web Presence:

BASHAR FOCUS

basharfocus.net
instagram.com/basharfocus/
youtube.com/@Basharfocus

MY ARTWORK

mikemckenneystudio.etsy.com
instagram.com/mikemckenneystudio/
youtube.com/@mikemckenneystudio5511
pinterest.com/mikemckenney8584/

Suggested Books to Assist with Transmutation

The following works have served as sacred mirrors, teachers, and tools of remembrance along my path. May they ignite something true within you, as they have for me.

Core Teachings and Metaphysical Foundations

- *A Course in Miracles* – Foundation for Inner Peace
- *The Kybalion* – Three Initiates
- *The Emerald Tablet: Alchemy for Personal Transformation* – Dennis William Hauck
- *A Return to Love: Reflections on the Principles of A Course in Miracles* – Marianne Williamson
- *The Alchemist* – Paulo Coelho
- *The Biology of Belief: Unleashing the Power of Consciousness, Matter & Miracles* – Bruce H. Lipton, Ph.D.

Embodied Awakening and Inner Healing

- *The Untethered Soul: The Journey Beyond Yourself* – Michael A. Singer
- *You Can Heal Your Life* – Louise Hay
- *The Power of Now: A Guide to Spiritual Enlightenment* – Eckhart Tolle
- *Becoming Supernatural: How Common People Are Doing the Uncommon* – Dr. Joe Dispenza

Feminine Wisdom and Sacred Archetypes

- *Women Who Run With the Wolves: Myths and Stories of the Wild Woman Archetype* – Clarissa Pinkola Estés

Spiritual Prosperity and Soul Purpose

- *The Seven Spiritual Laws of Success* – Deepak Chopra
- *Seat of the Soul* – Gary Zukav
- *Conversations with God: An Uncommon Dialogue (Book 1)* – Neale Donald Walsch

Photo Journal

Waffles (2021)

First Ayahuasca Ceremony (2021)

Feather in poncho, Hollywood, FL (2024)

Fermentation by LuRu (2024)

Cusco, Peru 2024

Cusco, Peru 2024

Sacred Valley, Peru 2024

Sacred Valley, Peru 2024

Sacred Valley, Peru 2024

Sacred Valley, Peru 2024

Aguas Calientes, Peru 2024

Machu Picchu, Peru 2024

Cusco, Peru 2024

Cusco, Peru 2024

Cusco, Peru 2024

Dania Beach, FL 2024

Van Gogh Café, Cusco, Peru 2025

Moray, Peru 2025

Salt Mines of Maras, Peru 2025

Hostel, Peru 2025

Cusco, Peru 2025

Fort Lauderdale, FL 2025

www.ingramcontent.com/pod-product-compliance
Lightning Source LLC
Chambersburg PA
CBHW070550050426
42450CB00011B/2791